Duden

Einfach klasse in

Englisch

Wissen • Üben • Testen

5. Klasse

2., neu bearbeitete und erweiterte Auflage

Dudenverlag
Mannheim • Leipzig • Wien • Zürich

Bibliografische Information der Deutschen Nationalbibliothek
Die Deutsche Nationalbibliothek verzeichnet diese Publikation in der Deutschen Nationalbibliografie; detaillierte bibliografische Daten sind im Internet über http://dnb.ddb.de abrufbar.

 D C B A

Redaktionelle Leitung Martin Bergmann
Redaktion Anika Donner, Martin Fruhstorfer
Autorinnen Birgit Hock, Meike Wolf
Sprecher Alison Ripier, Michael Shiels

Herstellung Annette Scheerer
Layout Horst Bachmann
Illustration Carmen Strzelecki
Umschlaggestaltung WohlgemuthPartners, Bremen
Umschlagabbildung Plainpicture

Satz Katrin Kleinschrot, Stuttgart
Druck und Bindung Offizin Andersen Nexö Leipzig GmbH
Printed in Germany

ISBN 978-3-411-72132-0

Inhaltsverzeichnis

5 Präpositionen

6 Wortstellung

7 Fragen

8 Zahlen, Uhrzeit und Datum

1 Substantive und Artikel

1.1 Substantive

Regelmäßige Pluralformen

Die regelmäßigen Pluralformen *(regular plural forms)* werden gebildet, indem man ein *-s* an das Substantiv (Nomen) anhängt.	one cat – two cat**s** one dog – two dog**s** one boy – two boy**s**
Endet ein Substantiv auf einem Zischlaut ([dʒ], [tʃ], [ks]) so hängt man ein *-es* an. Die Aussprache ist [ɪz].	one sandwich ['sænwɪtʃ] – two sandwich**es** ['sænwɪtʃɪz] one box [bɒks] – two box**es** ['bɒksɪz]
Endet ein Substantiv auf einem Konsonanten + *-y*, lautet die Pluralendung *-ies*.	one baby – two bab**ies** one family – two famil**ies** one hobby – two hobb**ies**
Bei manchen Substantiven auf *-f* oder *-fe* wird der Plural mit *-ves* gebildet.	one booksh**e**l**f** – two booksh**e**l**ves** one kni**fe** – two kni**ves**
Bestimmte Substantive auf *-o* hängen im Plural *-es* an.	tomat**o** – tomat**oes** potat**o** – potat**oes**

Unregelmäßige Pluralformen

Einige wenige Substantive haben unregelmäßige Pluralformen *(irregular plural forms)*, die du auswendig lernen musst.	man [mæn] – **men** [men] woman ['wʊmən] – **women** ['wɪmɪn] child [tʃaɪld] – **children** ['tʃɪldrən] foot [fʊt] – **feet** [fiːt] tooth [tuːθ] – **teeth** [tiːθ]

ÜBUNG 1 **Bilde den Plural der folgenden Substantive.**

class		house	
book		shoe	
page		scarf	
teacher		cat	
pupil		bird	
friend		dog	
table		tomato	
hobby		boy	
day		girl	

ÜBUNG 2 **In der Wortschlange haben sich einige Pluralwörter versteckt. Schreibe sie auf und ergänze die dazugehörigen Singulare.**

Plural	Singular

ÜBEN

ÜBUNG 3 **Sieh dir das Bild genau an und schreibe auf, was und wie viel davon sich auf Peters und Sues Schreibtisch befindet.**

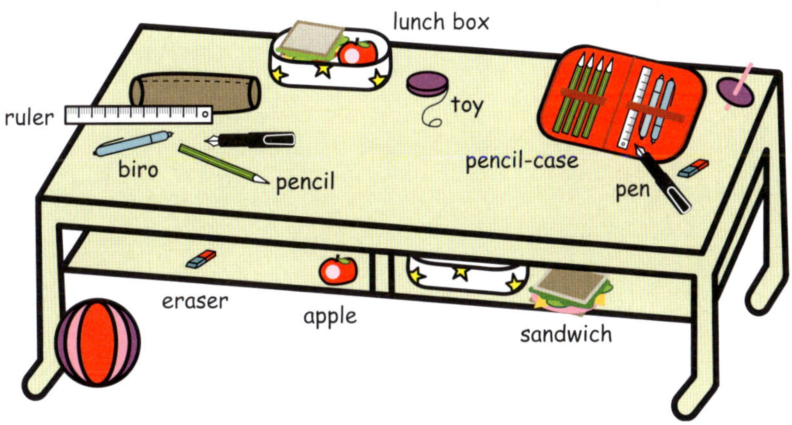

On Peter and Sue's desk are:

WISSEN

Ausspracheregeln
Bei der Aussprache der Substantive im Plural musst du aufpassen: Sie richtet sich nach der Wortendung im Singular.

Wird das Plural-*s* an einen weichen Konsonanten *(b, d, g, l, n, m)* oder an einen Vokal angehängt, so musst du es stimmhaft aussprechen. Dieses -*s* hört sich wie der Summlaut einer Biene an.	dog – dogs [gz] school bag – school bags [gz] classroom – classrooms [mz] pencil case – pencil cases [ɪz]
Wird das Plural-*s* an einen harten Konsonanten *(p, t, k)* oder einen Vokal, den man nicht ausspricht, angehängt, so musst du es stimmlos aussprechen. Dieses -*s* hört sich wie der Zischlaut einer Schlange an.	cat – cats [ts] group – groups [ps] book – books [ks] snake – snakes [ks]

ÜBEN

ÜBUNG 4 **Bilde den Plural der folgenden Wörter und sortiere sie je nach der Aussprache in die passende Spalte.**

house – friend – book – window – bed – chocolate – orange – banana – shop – snake – cage – watch

[z]	[ɪz]	[s]

ÜBUNG 5 **Höre dir Track 1 auf der CD an und setze die Substantive in der richtigen Form ein. Achte darauf, dass nicht alle Substantive im Plural stehen.**

1

Dear Sarah,

Thank you for your letter. I'm fine. How are you? You wanted to know what I do in my free time? Well, my favourite hobby is hockey. Two ______ train our team on Wednesday afternoons. We usually play two ______ on Saturdays. There are eleven ______ on each team and we all have hockey ______. But there is only one ______. Our players wear green ______ and we all have special ______. A lot of ______ and ______ come to watch the matches.

After the matches we often have dinner together. I usually eat two or three ______ and drink two small ______ of coke. I'm always very hungry after playing. Sometimes my mother brings two big ______. They are yummy!

What are your ______?

Hope to hear from you soon!

Yours, Andrew

1.2 Paarwörter und nicht zählbare Substantive

Paarwörter

Einige Substantive werden nur im Plural verwendet. Dazu gehören die Paarwörter *(pair nouns)*. Diese Substantive bezeichnen Dinge, die aus zwei gleichen Teilen bestehen.	trousers – Hose shorts – Shorts jeans – Jeans pyjamas – Schlafanzug glasses – Brille scissors – Schere
Bei Paarwörtern steht auch das Verb im Plural.	Your new trousers **look** great. My glasses **are** dirty. Where **are** my pyjamas?
Paarwörter können nicht mit *a / an* oder *one / two / three* verbunden werden. Will man ein Paarwort zählbar machen, so muss man es mit *a / one pair of, two pairs of, three pairs of* ... verbinden.	Have you got **a pair of** scissors? Shall I take **two pairs of** shorts? Don't take **three pairs of** jeans!

Nicht zählbare Substantive

Einige Wörter existieren nur im Singular. Es sind nicht zählbare Substantive *(uncountable nouns)*, die man nicht zählen und nicht in die Pluralform setzen kann. Diese Wörter musst du auswendig lernen.	food – Essen milk – Milch water – Wasser homework – Hausaufgaben bread – Brot tea – Tee music – Musik
Die nicht zählbaren Substantive können nicht mit *a / an* oder *one / two / three* verbunden werden. Will man sie zählbar machen, braucht man eine entsprechende Ergänzung.	I would like **a / one glass of** water. Could I have **two cups of** tea, please?

ÜBUNG 6 **Ergänze den folgenden Dialog.**

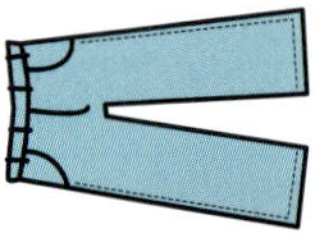

Sue: "Hi Kate! What are you doing?"

Kate: "Oh, I'm looking for ___ . What about you?"

Sue: "I need ___ for the summer."

Kate: "You're right. My old ___ are too small. I need a new pair, too."

Sue: "Shopping always makes me tired. Let's go and sit down somewhere."

Kate: "That's a good idea. Would you like ___ ?"

Sue: "No, I think I'll have ___ ."

Kate: "Me, too. Let's get ___ ___ at that tea room over there."

ÜBUNG 7 **Übersetze die folgenden Sätze ins Englische.**

Deine neue Brille ist hübsch.

___

Meine Hausaufgaben waren leicht.

___

Wo ist meine Jeans?

___

Ich habe keine Schere.

___

Peter hat zwei blaue Hosen.

___

Mein Pyjama ist zu klein.

___

1.3 Der Genitiv

Der *s*-Genitiv

Um auszudrücken, dass etwas oder jemand zu einer Person gehört, verwendet man den *s*-Genitiv. Dieser wird gebildet, indem man an das Substantiv einen Apostroph + *s* anhängt.	John**'s** dog Peter**'s** bike Clare**'s** birthday the boy**'s** computer (ein Junge)
Wenn etwas **mehreren** Personen gehört, hängt man nur einen Apostroph an die Pluralform an.	the boys' computer (mehrere Jungen) the teachers' lessons the pupils' English teacher
Bei den unregelmäßigen Pluralformen hängt man einen Apostroph + *s* an.	men**'s** shoes – women**'s** clothes – children**'s** games
Merke: Gehört etwas zwei Personen, so steht das *'s* nur einmal.	Amy and George**'s** cat
Aufgepasst: Steht am Ende eines Substantivs ein *s*, musst du genau überlegen, wie es geschrieben wird. Es gibt ▪ das Plural-*s*: Hier setzt du keinen Apostroph! ▪ das Genitiv-*s* bei Substantiven im Singular: Hier steht ein Apostroph vor dem *s*. ▪ den Genitiv bei Substantiven im Plural: Hier steht der Apostroph hinter dem Plural-*s*.	There are 12 girl**s** and 11 boy**s** in my class. We have three car**s** at home. My brother**'s** car is blue. My sister**'s** car is old. My parent**s'** car is new. My grandparent**s'** house is very small.

Die *of*-Fügung

Um auszudrücken, dass etwas oder jemand zu einer Sache gehört, verwendet man die *of*-Fügung.	the colour **of** your jeans the first day **of** the week the pages **of** the book

ÜBUNG 8 **Bilde den Genitiv Plural.**

Singular	Plural
the boy's class	the boys' class
the school's buildings	
the man's job	
the girl's room	
the child's toys	
the woman's hair	
the family's cars	
the pupil's teacher	

ÜBUNG 9 **Übersetze die rot markierten Satzteile.**

Hast du Julias und Emilys neuen Hund gesehen?

Du kannst dir Lucys Bücher ausleihen.

Das Auto der Johnsons ist nagelneu.

Der Lehrer der Schüler kommt aus Kanada.

Glaubst du, Mr Smiths Sohn kommt in unsere Klasse?

Die Farbe deiner Augen ist schwer zu bestimmen.

Der Fernseher der Familie ist schon seit Wochen kaputt.

Das Ende des Spiels steht unmittelbar bevor.

ÜBUNG 10 Folge den Linien und schreibe auf, wem oder zu wem etwas gehört.

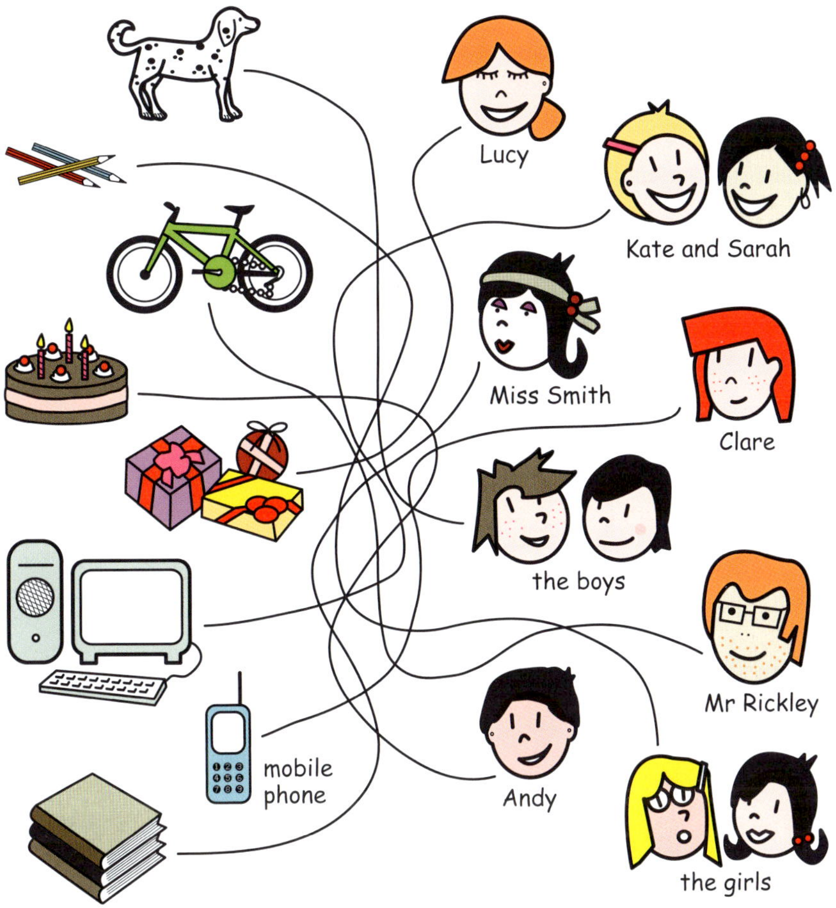

the boys' dog,

ÜBEN

1.4 Der Artikel

Der bestimmte Artikel

Im Deutschen kennst du die bestimmten Artikel *der, die und das*. Im Englischen gibt es nur *einen* bestimmten Artikel *(definite article): the.*	Where is **the** new teacher? **The** boys in my class are nice, but I don't like **the** girls.
Im Deutschen gibt es einige Wendungen, bei denen wir keinen Artikel benutzen. Im Englischen muss er aber stehen.	He plays **the** piano / **the** drums / **the** guitar. (Er spielt Klavier / Schlagzeug / Gitarre.) They often listen to **the** radio. (Sie hören oft Radio.)
Genauso gibt es Wendungen, in denen wir im Deutschen einen Artikel verwenden, wohingegen im Englischen keiner steht. Zum Beispiel - bei Straßennamen, - in bestimmten Wendungen.	He lives **in** Hill Road (in der Hill Road). Peter doesn't want to go **to bed,** but Sue is already **in bed** (ins Bett, im Bett). What's **on TV** tonight (im Fernsehen)? I'm **at school.** My dad's **at work** (in der Schule, bei der Arbeit). We usually go **by train / bus / car** (mit dem Zug / Bus / Auto). Let's meet **before / after breakfast / lunch / dinner** (vor / nach dem Frühstück / dem Mittagessen / dem Abendessen).

Der unbestimmte Artikel

Aus dem Deutschen kennst du die unbestimmten Artikel *ein* und *eine*. Im Englischen lautet der unbestimmte Artikel *(indefinite article) a* bzw. *an*.	**a** tree – **an** apple
Beginnt das Bezugswort mit einem **Konsonanten**, so verwendet man *a*.	**a h**ouse – **a b**edroom – **a k**itchen – **a r**ed apple
Beginnt das Bezugswort mit einem **Vokal**, so steht *an*. *Achtung:* Wird das *u* jedoch wie [juː] ausgesprochen, so steht *a*.	**an u**mbrella – **an a**nimal – **an o**ld dog **a u**niform ['juːnɪfɔːm] – **a u**nit ['juːnɪt]

WISSEN

ÜBUNG 11 **Setze den unbestimmten Artikel *a* oder *an* vor die Substantive.**

___ animal	___ orange
___ fish	___ banana
___ old cat	___ apple
___ mouse	___ idea
___ elephant	___ easy exercise
___ uniform	___ hobby
___ uncle	___ interesting hobby

ÜBUNG 12 **Sarah schreibt Andrew eine Karte aus den Sommerferien. Füge den bestimmten Artikel *the* überall dort in die Lücken ein, wo er notwendig ist. Tipp: Bei fünf Lücken musst du nichts einsetzen!**

Dear Andrew,
How are you? I'm fine. Italy is great. ___
weather is fantastic. In the morning we usually
have a big breakfast. After ___ breakfast we
walk to ___ beach and go for a swim in ___
sea. In the afternoon we sometimes go to little
towns by ___ bus. ___ shops are quite nice
and ___ clothes are a bit cheaper than in Eng-
land. We usually sit down in one of ___ cafés
and have some ice cream. After ___ supper we
often play ___ cards or listen to ___ radio.
Sometimes we play ___ table tennis. What are
you doing in your holidays?
Love, Sarah

Andrew Boyle
6 Blundell Street
London N798BK
Great Britain

ÜBEN

WISSEN

Berufe
Vor Berufsbezeichnungen verwenden wir im Deutschen keinen Artikel.
Im Englischen muss jedoch der unbestimmte Artikel stehen.

Ich bin Bäcker. – I'm **a** baker.
Miss Wilkinson ist Lehrerin. – Miss Wilkinson is **a** teacher.
Mein Vater ist kein Metzger, er ist Ingenieur. – My father is not **a** butcher, he's **an** engineer.

ÜBUNG 13 **Tom und John unterhalten sich über Johns morgigen Geburtstag. Setze den bestimmten oder unbestimmten Artikel in die Lücken ein. Tipp: Bei manchen Lücken musst du nichts einsetzen!**

Tom: "Hey John, it's your birthday tomorrow, isn't it?"

John: "Yes, it is. I usually have ______ big party. ______ party takes place in our garage because ______ garage is big enough for all of us. Why don't you come, too?"

Tom: "Thanks for ______ invitation. But I'm sorry, I can't come. I have to look after my brother because my mother is at ______ work. She's ______ nurse."

John: "What a shame! It's always great fun. After ______ school most of my friends come to my parents' house in ______ Redwood Road. We usually have ______ yummy birthday cake. Then I open ______ presents and after that we play games."

Tom: "My aunt usually gives me cool things for my birthday. I sometimes get ______ new computer games from her. Do you know what you will get?"

John: "No, I don't. I would love to have ______ new mountain bike. ______ old bike is broken; but ______ mountain bikes are very expensive."

Tom: "Well, good luck! I hope you'll have ______ wonderful birthday party. Maybe I can come over when my mother's back from ______ work."

John: "That's great. See you tomorrow! Bye."

ÜBEN

Klassenarbeit 1

45 Minuten

AUFGABE 1 **Wie lautet die Pluralform der folgenden Substantive?**

man	child
sandwich	knife
baby	box
boy	potato
woman	house
class	tooth

AUFGABE 2 **Bilde Sätze mit den Bestandteilen aus den Wolken. Vorsicht! Erinnere dich daran, wie man Paarwörter und nicht zählbare Substantive zählbar macht (↑ Kap. 1.2).**

1.

I've got

2x pyjamas – 3x jeans –
1x scissors – 2x water

2.

My trousers – The glass –
My new glasses – The two cups of tea

are / is

nice – empty – dirty – hot

AUFGABE 3 **Bens Computerprogramm hat einen Virus; es hat die Apostrophe, das Plural-*s* und teilweise das Genitiv-s verschluckt. Füge sie an der richtigen Stelle ein.**

To: Brad.Stevens@coolmail.com¶
From: BenWalker@ballyhoo.com¶
Sent: Monday, July 27th, 2009, 11:10 a.m.¶
Subject: Our new house¶
¶
Hi Brad,¶
We moved into our new house. It is fantastic. Now I have my own
little room. My two brother   Tim and Joe also have their own rooms.
But my two sister   share a big room. My sister   room is next to
mine and my parent   bedroom is also on the first floor.¶
My brother   rooms are downstairs. Blacky   basket is in the hall
right next to Tim and Joe   rooms, so he doesn't have to sleep in
the garage. My dad   office and my mum   reading room are also on
the ground floor. So, now there's enough room for everyone. What's
more, the garage is big enough for my parent   car, my brother
bikes and the children   toys. Come and visit us! We'll have a big
party next month. Hope to see you soon.¶
Yours, Ben

AUFGABE 4 **Übersetze die folgenden Sätze ins Englische. Achte dabei besonders auf die Verwendung der bestimmten und unbestimmten Artikel!**

Mrs Stevens hat ein altes Auto, aber Mr Stevens hat ein neues Fahrrad.

Das neue Haus der Stevens befindet sich am Ende der Mill Road.

Nach dem Frühstück fährt Ben mit dem Bus zur Schule.

Bens Vater ist Architekt *(architect)*, seine Mutter ist Zahnärztin *(dentist)*.

Klassenarbeit 2

45 Minuten

AUFGABE 5 **Wie lautet die Pluralform der folgenden Substantive?**

watch		milk	
hobby		mobile phone	
bus		food	
lesson		fish	
photo		desk	
party		people	

AUFGABE 6 **Setze jeweils den richtigen unbestimmten Artikel (*a / an*) in die Lücke.**

	old house		nice party
	English girl		attractive teacher
	good book		answer to my question
	hour		young dog

AUFGABE 7 **Marys Kleiderschrank ist gut gefüllt. Schreibe vollständige Sätze in dein Übungsheft und achte darauf, dass die Pluralformen nicht nur richtig sind, sondern auch mit den richtigen Mengenangaben versehen werden.**

Beispiel: shoes (5) → Mary has got **five pairs of shoes** in her wardrobe.

blue-jeans (5) – T-shirt (11) – hat (1) – sunglasses (2) – socks (8) – dress (5) – pyjamas (4) – shorts (3) – swimsuit (1) – bikini (2)

AUFGABE 8 **Schreibe in dein Übungsheft jeweils drei Sachen, die ...**

1. man zählen kann.
2. du in der Schule siehst.
3. zu einem Haus gehören.
4. der Fortbewegung dienen.
5. du dir zum Geburtstag wünschst.

AUFGABE 9 **Vervollständige die Sätze, indem du einen bestimmten oder unbestimmten Artikel einsetzt.**

Make sandwich, please!

May I have cup of tea, please?

Bring milk here, please!

Can you get me phone, please?

Is this empty box?

Now it's your turn, Simon. Throw ball!

AUFGABE 10 **Anne und Lilly lieben süße Kuchen. Beim letzten Backen haben die beiden leider etwas gekleckert, manche Wörter des Rezepts sind deshalb nicht mehr richtig lesbar. Bessere das Rezept aus.**

Chocolate Muffins

makes 12–15 medium size muffi

You need:

2 eg

1 cup sug

1 cup flou

6 teaspo cocoa powder

2 teaspo baking powder

1 teaspo vanilla essence

2/3 cu milk

2/3 cu butter

4 ounc semisweet chocolate chi

Preheat oven to 180° C. Grease *(fette ein)* 12–15 medium muffin ti *(Förmchen)*. Beat the eg with sug , mix with flou , cocoa powd , baking powder, vanilla and mil . Stir *(umrühren)* with melted butte . Add *(hinzugeben)* chocolate chips and bake for 20 minut .

TESTEN

2 Pronomen

2.1 Personalpronomen

Substantive können durch **Personalpronomen *(personal pronouns)*** ersetzt werden.	**Peter** goes to school. → **He** goes to school.
Bei Personen und Haustieren, die einen Namen haben, verwendet man die Pronomen *he* oder *she*.	Mrs O'Connor is a teacher.→ She is a teacher. Cheeky is our dog. → He is our dog.
Aufgepasst: Bei Gegenständen und anderen Tieren verwendet man *it*.	The TV is broken (kaputt). → It is broken. This dog is big. → It is big.
Nach den Personalpronomen in der **Subjektform** fragt man mit „wer?". Sie stehen hier mit dem Verb *to be (sein):*	**Ich** bin eure Lehrerin („wer?") – **I** am your teacher.

Langform	Kurzform		
***I** am*	***I'**m*	*ich bin*	I am / I'm a good pupil.
***you** are*	***you'**re*	*du bist*	You are / You're my best friend.
***he / she / it** is*	***he'**s / **she'**s / **it'**s*	*er / sie / es ist*	She is / She's swimming in the swimming pool.
***we** are*	***we'**re*	*wir sind*	We are / We're doing our homework.
***you** are*	***you'**re*	*ihr seid*	You are / You're looking good today.
***they** are*	***they'**re*	*sie sind*	They are / They're English.

Nach den Personalpronomen in der **Objektform** fragt man im Deutschen mit „wem?" oder „wen?".	Ich rede mit **ihm** („wem?"). → I'm talking to **him.** Ich mag **ihn** („wen?"). → I like **him.**

me	*mir, mich*	Please give me the pencil!
you	*dir, dich*	She likes you!
him / her / it	*ihm, ihn / ihr, sie / ihm, es*	There, the bird! Can you see it?
us	*uns*	Show us your picture, please.
you	*euch, Ihnen, Sie*	Let me help you.
them	*ihnen, sie*	I can call them later.

ÜBUNG 1 **Sue schreibt ihrem Brieffreund Tim einen Brief, in dem sie ihm von ihrer Familie erzählt. Füge die Subjektform des Personalpronomens in die Lücken ein.**

Hi Tim,

I'm going to tell you something about my family. My name is Sue. ______ am eleven years old. My dad is called Adam. ______ is 40 years old. My mother's name is Carole. ______ is 36 years old. ______ are both teachers. ______ have two brothers. ______ are six and eight years old. We live in a very busy street but ______ have a nice garden. ______ is quite big. ______ can play football there. ______ can visit me here. ______ are always welcome.

Lots of love,

Sue

WISSEN

Das Personalpronomen *you*
Das englische *you are* hat im Deutschen drei Entsprechungen: *du bist* und *ihr seid* sowie die Höflichkeitsform *Sie sind*. Die deutschen Pronomen *du, ihr* und *Sie* werden also alle mit *you* übersetzt.

Du bist spät.	**You are** late.
Ihr seid sehr nett.	**You are** very kind.
Sie sind unsere neue Englischlehrerin.	**You are** our new English teacher.

ÜBUNG 2 **Ersetze die roten Satzteile durch Personalpronomen in der Objektform.**

The teacher tells the children to be quiet. ______

The teacher is giving Sarah a book. ______

Can you help Peter? ______

Please give the book to your sister. ______

The neighbours are helping our family. ______

Can you ask Peter and Sarah? ______

I love to play with my toy car. ______

These flowers are for Mrs Wood. ______

WISSEN +

Fehlerquelle: *er – sie – es* bei Sachen
Im Deutschen können Gegenstände maskulin (männlich), feminin (weiblich) oder Neutrum (sächlich) sein.

der Bus
die Tür
das Schloss

Je nach dem grammatischen Geschlecht wird im Deutschen auch das **Pronomen** gebildet:
- Subjektform: *er, sie, es*
- Objektform: *ihm, ihn, ihr, sie* oder *es*

Im Englischen hingegen steht bei Gegenständen immer das Personalpronomen ***it.***

Personalpronomen in der Subjektform:
Der Bus fährt um 10:30 Uhr. **Er** hat Verspätung. – **The bus** leaves at 10:30. **It** is late.
Die Tür ist offen. Mach **sie** bitte zu. **The door** is open. Please close **it.**

Personalpronomen in der Objektform:
Der Bus kommt. Ich kann **ihn** sehen. – The bus is coming. I can see **it**.
Ist das deine neue Schultasche? Zeig **sie** mir. – Is this your new school bag? Show **it** to me.

ÜBUNG 3 **Im folgenden Dialog sind einige Personalpronomen in der Subjekt- und Objektform falsch verwendet. Höre dir Track 2 auf der CD an und verbessere sie, indem du die falschen Personalpronomen durchstreichst und die richtigen darüberschreibst.**

ACHTUNG FEHLER

2

Ann: "Hey Kate, there is a new boy in our class. Have you seen ~~her~~ him?"

Kate: "No, me haven't. What is he like? Where is him from?"

Ann: "It seems very nice. His family moved from Nottingham to London three weeks ago. He's got a sister, too, but I haven't met him. Them live near we. Let we visit they."

Kate: "Me don't know. I don't know he."

Ann: "Don't be silly. He invited my. I'm sure it can come, too."

Kate: "Okay. Let's go."

ÜBEN

2.2 Possessivbegleiter und Possessivpronomen

Possessivbegleiter

Possessivbegleiter *(possessive determiners)* zeigen an, wem oder zu wem etwas gehört. Sie stehen direkt vor Substantiven.

Where is **my** schoolbag?
It's in **your** bedroom.

my	*mein*	This is **my** dog.
your	*dein*	**Your** sister is very pretty.
his	*sein*	**His** car is old.
her	*ihr*	**Her** suitcase is big.
its	*sein*	The dog carries **its** food bowl.
our	*unser*	Where is **our** hotel?
your	*euer, Ihr*	This is **your** teacher.
their	*ihr*	Mr Smith is **their** father.

Merke: Wenn etwas zu Sachen oder Tieren gehört, die keinen Namen haben, so verwendet man *its*.

The cat is playing with **its** ball.
The bird is sitting in **its** cage.

Possessivbegleiter stehen im Gegensatz zum Deutschen auch bei Körperteilen und Kleidungsstücken, wo sie im Deutschen oft nicht notwendig sind.

He broke **his** left arm. (Er hat sich **den** linken Arm gebrochen.)
Please take off **your** shoes. (Zieh bitte **die** Schuhe aus.)

Possessivpronomen

Die **Possessivpronomen *(possessive pronouns)*** zeigen ebenfalls an, wem etwas gehört. Im Unterschied zu den Possessivbegleitern stehen sie jedoch allein und ersetzen das Substantiv.

mine	*meiner, meine, mein[e]s*	This shirt is **mine,** isn't it?
yours	*deiner, ...*	Yes, it's **yours.**
his/hers	*seiner, ... / ihrer, ...*	No, it's **his.**
		It can't be **hers.**
ours	*unserer, ...*	Maybe it's **ours.**
yours	*euerer, ...*	Hey, Tony and Bob, is it **yours?**
theirs	*ihrer, ...*	I think it's **theirs.**

ÜBUNG 4 **Ersetze die roten Satzteile mit dem passenden Possessivbegleiter.**

Peter's ______ bike		my mother's ______ shoes	
Kate and Sue's ______ basketball		the horse's ______ saddle	

WISSEN

Vorsicht: Verwechslungsgefahr! **It's** und **its** werden zwar gleich ausgesprochen, haben aber unterschiedliche Bedeutungen. Wenn die Kurzform von *it is (es ist)* gemeint ist, schreibst du **it's**. Geht es um den Possessivbegleiter, der anzeigt, so schreibst du **its**.	The cat eats **its** food. *Aber:* **It's** cold outside.
Genauso aufpassen musst du bei der Schreibweise von **your** (Possessivbegleiter, *dein*) und **you're** (Kurzform von *you are: du bist*).	Is this **your** watch? *Aber:* **You're** late.
Auch **his** (Possessivbegleiter) und **he's** (Kurzform von *he is: er ist*) darfst du nicht verwechseln.	This is **his** room. *Aber:* **He's** my brother.
Bei dem Possessivbegleiter **their** gibt es sogar zwei Formen, die zwar ähnlich ausgesprochen werden, aber andere Bedeutungen haben: **they're** ist die Kurzform von *they are (sie sind)*; **there** bedeutet *da* oder *dort*.	Bob and Adam are riding **their** bikes over **there.** *Aber:* **They're** very young.

ÜBUNG 5 **Höre dir Track 3 auf der CD an und füge die fehlenden Possessivbegleiter und Possessivpronomen in die Lücken ein. Achtung: Bei einigen Lücken brauchst du zusätzlich eine Form von *to be*! (↑ Kap. 3.2).**

3

1. Tracy: "Mark, where is ______ schoolbag?"
   Mark: "I don't know. There is one over there. Is that ______?"
   Tracy: "Yes, that's ______!"
2. Mark: "Hey Wendy, is this ______ new cat?"
   Wendy: "Yes, ______ cute, isn't it? This is ______ new toy. ______ a little plastic mouse."
3. Betty: "Andy and Brian are twins. ______ sisters Hannah and Clare are over there."
   Joe: "Are they twins, too?"
   Betty: "No, ______ not."

ÜBEN

ÜBUNG 6 **Schau dir das Bild genau an und schreibe auf, was du siehst. Verwende dabei Possessivbegleiter.**

Look!

There is Peter with his dog.

There

There

There

There

There

There

ÜBEN

WISSEN

Das deutsche *ihr* – *her* oder *their*?
Bei der Übersetzung des deutschen Wortes *ihr* musst du besonders aufmerksam sein. Gehört eine Sache einer Besitzerin (also Singular feminin), so musst du ***her*** verwenden. Gehört eine Sache mehreren Besitzern (also Plural), so verwendest du ***their***.

Mrs Hunt sucht **ihr** Auto (das Auto gehört Mrs Hunt *allein*). – Mrs Hunt is looking for **her** car.
Mr und Mrs Grant suchen **ihr** Auto (das Auto gehört *beiden*). – Mr and Mrs Grant are looking for **their** car.

Das deutsche sie – *she, her, they, them oder you?*
Das Wörtchen *sie* ist besonders gemein. Je nachdem, wer mit *sie* gemeint ist, gibt es fünf Möglichkeiten, es ins Englische zu übersetzen.

- Singular feminin (Subjektform): **Sie** (Sarah) öffnet die Tür. – **She** is opening the door.
- Singular feminin (Objektform): Ich mag **sie** (Sarah). – I like **her**.
- Plural (Subjektform): **Sie** (Sarah und Peter) schließen die Fenster. – **They** are closing the windows.
- Plural (Objektform): Ich frage **sie** (die Eltern). – I ask **them.**
- Höflichkeitsform: Sind **Sie** Mrs Grey? – Are **you** Mrs Grey?

ÜBUNG 7 **Wähle den passenden Possessivbegleiter und füge ihn ein.**

Carole is looking for ________ (his / her / its) shoes. ________ (his / her / their) brother is helping her. They are looking in ________ (our / their / her) bedrooms and in ________ (her / your / their) parents' bedroom, but they can't find them anywhere. Carole tells ________ (her / his / our) mother: "We're looking for ________ (their / my / our) shoes!" – "Ask ________ (her / his / your) grandpa. He's in ________ (her / their / his) room. Maybe he knows where your shoes are."

ÜBUNG 8 **Ersetze die rot markierten Wörter durch die englischen Pronomen.**

Sie (die Johnsons) haben ein großes Haus. ________

Ich besuche sie (meine Großeltern) jedes Wochenende. ________

Entschuldigung, kennen Sie den Weg zum Bahnhof? ________

ÜBEN

2.3 Demonstrativpronomen

Mithilfe von **Demonstrativpronomen *(demonstrative pronouns)*** weist man auf etwas hin. Sie lauten im

Singular:	**Plural:**
this	***these***
that	***those***

"**This** is my football." (dieser Fußball hier)

This und *these* werden für Personen oder Dinge verwendet, die sich in der näheren Umgebung des Sprechers befinden.

"**These** muffins are delicious."

That und *those* werden für Personen oder Dinge verwendet, die sich in weiterer Entfernung befinden. Bei diesen Demostrativpronomen steht oft *over there*.

"**That's** my new bike over there." (das Fahrrad dort drüben)

"Can you see **those** people over there? They're my friends."

Demonstrativpronomen können vor einem Substantiv oder alleine stehen.

Can I read **this** book?
That's my book.
These shoes are mine.
Those are your shoes.

ÜBUNG 9 **Ergänze das jeweils fehlende Demonstrativpronomen im Singular oder Plural.**

this car	↔	______	cars
______	pet	↔	those pets
that girl	↔	______	girls
______	boy	↔	these boys
that man	↔	______	men
______	child	↔	these children
those bikes	↔	______	bike
______	chairs	↔	this chair

ÜBUNG 10 **Füge die passenden Demonstrativpronomen ein.**

“______ is my English book here and ______ is your maths book over there.”

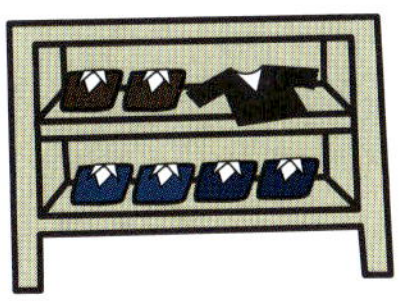

“Nick, do you like ______ jumpers here better than ______ over there?” –
“I don’t know, mum, but I like ______ shirts over there.”

“Should I buy ______ expensive CD or ______ two cheap cassettes?”

ÜBUNG 11 **Hannah kauft Obst und Gemüse auf dem Markt ein. Schau dir das Bild an und füge anschließend die Demonstrativpronomen in den Dialog ein. Achte dabei darauf, ob die Dinge näher oder weiter entfernt vom Sprecher sind.**

Hannah: "Good morning, Mrs Rose."
Mrs Rose: "Good morning, my dear."
Hannah: "Could I have one kilo of potatoes, please?"
Mrs Rose: "Sure. Would you like ______ new potatoes here or ______ sweet potatoes over there?"
Hannah: "______ new potatoes, please. Are ______ oranges sweet?"
Mrs Rose: "Oh, they're okay. But ______ tangerines *(Mandarinen)* over there are lovely."
Hannah: "I'll have six tangerines then, and ______ watermelon next to them. What is ______ round fruit here?"
Mrs Rose: "Oh, ______ is a mango. Try it! Mangos taste delicious."
Hannah: "Okay, one mango, please. Could I also have a few of ______ bananas over there?"
Mrs Rose: "Of course. Anything else?"
Hannah: "No, thank you very much. That's fine. Bye."
Mrs Rose: "Have a nice day. Bye."

ÜBEN

Klassenarbeit 1

45 Minuten

AUFGABE 1 **Thomas erzählt seinem Vater von seinem ersten Schultag in der neuen Schule. Fülle die Lücken mit den fehlenden Pronomen.**

Mr Simpson: "Hi Thomas, how was the first day at ________ (deiner) new school?"

Thomas: "Hi dad, ________ (meine) new school is not too bad. My classmates are friendly and ________ (unser) classroom is nice, too."

Mr Simpson: "What does it look like?"

Thomas: "Well, ________ (es) is a big room with lots of posters. ________ (Seine) windows are also big, so we can look outside when the lessons are boring."

Mr Simpson: "Oh dear. Are ________ (deine) new teachers so boring?"

Thomas: "I don't know yet. Our English teacher, Miss Walker, is nice. ________ (ihre) two sons are in ________ (meiner) class as well. ________ (Ihr) table is next to ________ (meinem)."

Mr Simpson: „Well, you must be hungry. ________ (dein) dinner is on the kitchen table."

AUFGABE 2 **Trage die fehlenden Pronomen in die Tabelle ein.**

		Personalpronomen (Subjektform)	Personalpronomen (Objektform)	Possessivbegleiter
Singular	1. Person	I	me	my
	2. Person			
	3. Person			
Plural	1. Person			
	2. Person			
	3. Person			

AUFGABE 3 **Wie lauten die roten Personalpronomen in der richtigen Übersetzung? Überlege, ob du die Subjekt- oder die Objektform benötigst.**

Kannst du mich anrufen? ____

Ich suche Emma und Tony. Hast du sie gesehen? ____

Ich glaube, sie sind schon nach Hause gegangen. ____

Können Sie mir sagen, wann der Bus nach Windsor fährt? ____

Ist Sue hier? Ja, sie ist dort drüben. ____

Gibst du mir bitte die Butter? ____

Wir sind neu. Kannst du uns helfen? ____

Das ist unser Klassenraum. ____

AUFGABE 4 **Füge die fehlenden Pronomen ein.**

1. Look, the Millers! ____ are our new neighbours. ____ house is next to ours. I'm baking a cake for ____.
2. Lisa: "Peter, is this ____ eraser?" – Peter: "Yes, can ____ give it to me?" – Lisa: "Is it really ____?"
3. I'm looking for ____ pencil case, but ____ can't find it. Can you help ____?
4. I found a hedgehog *(Igel)* in the garden. I can show ____ to you, but ____ is very shy. ____ spines *(Stacheln)* feel strange, don't they?
5. "Who is ____ man over there?" – "I don't know ____."

AUFGABE 5 **Übersetze die roten Satzteile ins Englische.**

Ich bat sie (meine Geschwister) ____ um Hilfe. Bitte lasse den Kuchen stehen. Das ist unserer ____. John brach sich beim Fußballspielen das Bein ____. Wo ist euer Lehrer ____? Hier ist ein Geldbeutel. Ist das deiner ____? Mike und John feiern ihre Geburtstage ____ gemeinsam. Die Maus frisst ihren Käse ____. Ms Williams hat ihre Tasche ____ verloren.

TESTEN

Klassenarbeit 2

45 Minuten

AUFGABE 6 **Ersetze die unterstrichenen Namen oder Substantive durch Personalpronomen.**

Anne usually eats cornflakes for breakfast. ______ usually eats cornflakes for breakfast.

Bill has got a red car. ______ has got a red car.

Mr Ledbetter teaches English. ______ teaches English.

My Mum and Dad live in New Zealand. ______ live in New Zealand.

The cat has a broken leg. ______ has a broken leg.

I am a musician. ______ name is Danny.

AUFGABE 7 **Hier siehst du einen Ausschnitt aus dem Stammbaum der Familie Miller. Setze die richtigen Personalpronomen ein.**

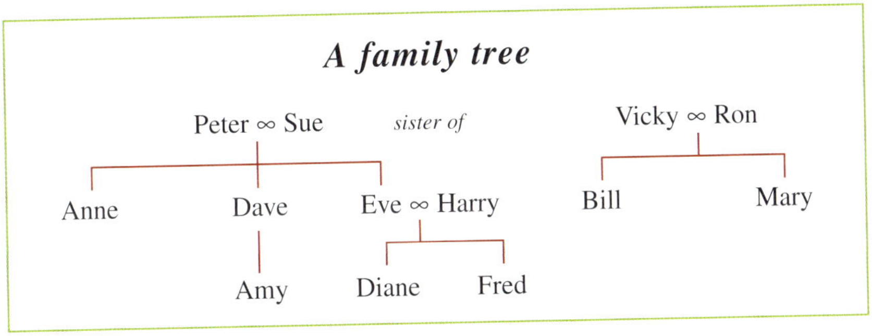

Peter is married to Sue. Sue is ______ wife.

Anne and Dave are Peter's children. ______ are brother and sister.

Eve is Anne's sister. ______ has got a brother, too.

Dave is not married, but ______ has a daughter called Amy.

Vicky is Sue's sister. Ron is ______ husband.

Bill and Mary are brother and sister. ______ are cousins of Anne, Dave and Eve.

Eve is married. Harry is ______ husband.

Sue is a grandmother, too. ______ grandchildren are Amy, Diane and Fred.

AUFGABE 8 **Familie Miller macht Urlaub in London. Ständig stellen sie neue Fragen an ihren Reiseführer. Aus den Antworten kannst du erschließen, ob du das Demonstrativpronomen im Singular *(that)* oder im Plural *(those)* einsetzen musst.**

What is that red thing? – It's a telephone box.

What is ________ ? – It's a museum.

Who are ________ ? –They are police officers.

Who are ________ ? – They are school children wearing a uniform.

What is ________ ? – It's Buckingham Palace.

Who are ________ ? – They are Beefeaters, guarding the Tower of London.

What is ________ ? – It's a bus-stop.

AUFGABE 9 ***This / that – these / those*. Setze ein.**

________ is a new car, but ________ over there are very old cars.

________ is an English book, but ________ over there is a German youth magazine.

What's ________ building over there?

________ cake here is for grandmother's birthday, but ________ muffins here are for you.

AUFGABE 10 **Übersetze. Schreibe in dein Übungsheft.**

Ich frage meine Mutter um Hilfe.
Können Sie mir sagen, wie ich zum Bahnhof komme?
Dieser Hund ist lästig *(annoying)*, die kleinen Katzen dort aber sind niedlich *(cute)*.
Wie groß bist du?
Ellen ist nicht zu Hause. Sie ist im Krankenhaus.
Unsere Nachbarn haben drei kleine Kinder.

Verben und Hilfsverben

3.1 Verben

Verben *(verbs)* sind Tätigkeitswörter. Sie geben an, was geschieht oder was jemand tut.	It **rains** a lot in England. Sue **likes** football. We often **swim** in the sea.
Beim Verwenden von Verben musst du aus der Grundform eine Personalform bilden.	to rain – it **rains** to like – she **likes** to swim – we **swim**
Es gibt drei Arten von Verben: ■ **Vollverben *(full verbs)***: Die meisten Verben sind Vollverben. Das bedeutet, sie stehen als einziges Verb im Satz.	I **read** a lot of books. My brother often **listens** to music. My dad **reads** his newspaper every day.
■ **Hilfsverben *(auxiliary verbs)*:** *Do* wird in Fragen, Kurzantworten und Verneinungen als Hilfsverb benötigt. Es steht dann in Verbindung mit einem Vollverb. *Be* wird im *present progressive* (↑ Kap. 4.2) als Hilfsverb verwendet. Auch die Form von *be* steht dann in Verbindung mit einem Vollverb + *-ing*.	**Do** you often go to the cinema? – Yes, I **do.**/ No, I **don't.** My mother **doesn't** watch television very often. Mrs Anderson **is** closing the window. **Are** you waiting for your teacher?
■ **modale Hilfsverben *(modal auxiliaries)***: *Can* (können, dürfen) und *must* (müssen) sind modale Hilfsverben. Sie stehen meist in Verbindung mit einem Vollverb.	**Can** you close the door, please? Tony **can** sing very well. You **must** tidy your room today.

ÜBUNG 1 **Unterstreiche die Vollverben im folgenden Text.**

My parents, my brothers and I often go to the zoo on Sundays. We always watch the monkeys and sometimes we give them bananas. Afterwards we walk over to the penguins. They are so cute *(süß)*. At three o'clock the zookeepers feed *(füttern)* the elephants. They are fantastic. I just love them. If we don't go to the zoo, I usually stay at home and read. I like detective stories and love stories. My brothers read lots of comics. I can sometimes borrow *(leihen)* them.

ÜBUNG 2 **Unterstreiche die Verbformen im Dialog. Dazu gehören die Vollverben, Hilfsverben und modalen Hilfsverben.**

John: "Alex, do you know where my English book is?"

Alex: "No, sorry, I don't. Do you need it?"

John: "Yes, I must do my homework."

Alex: "How boring! Why don't you do it tomorrow?"

John: "I can't do it tomorrow because it's mum's birthday. I need the book today."

Alex: "Okay. You can have mine."

John: "Thanks a lot. That's very kind of you."

ÜBUNG 3 **Suche das passende Verb aus den Wolken aus und füge es in der richtigen Form im *simple present* (↑ Kap. 4.1) ein.**

be — do — get up — start — like — hate — play — have got

My sister often _____ with our dog.

I always _____ my homework in the afternoon.

I _____ chocolate.

Some children _____ school.

Sarah usually _____ at 7 o'clock.

School _____ at 8 o'clock.

Our maths teacher _____ always late.

Clare _____ two brothers and one sister.

3.2 Das Vollverb *be*

Das Verb *be* bedeutet *sein*. In **bejahten Aussagesätzen** der Gegenwart kann es in der Lang- und der Kurzform stehen: **Langform** / **Kurzform** *I **am*** / *I'**m*** *You **are*** / *You'**re*** *He / she / it **is*** / *He / she / it'**s*** *Achtung:* *You are* kann im Deutschen *du bist*, *ihr seid* und *Sie sind* heißen (↑ S. 22).	I **am / I'm** your brother. You **are / you're** my sister. She **is / she's** good at English. We **are / we're** on holiday. You **are / you're** my classmates. They **are / they're** happy.
Bei einem **verneinten Aussagesatz** der Gegenwart mit dem Verb *be* wird ein *not* hinter *am*, *are* oder *is* gesetzt. Auch hier gibt es Lang- und Kurzformen. **Langform** / **Kurzform** *I **am not*** / *I'**m not*** *You **are not*** / *You **aren't*** *Achtung:* Bei der Verneinung im Präsens gibt es zwei Kurzformen. *Ausnahme:* *I am not* wird immer zu *I'm not*.	I **am not / I'm not** your brother. You **are not / you aren't** my sister. She **is not / she isn't** good at English. We **are not / we aren't** on holiday. You **are not / you aren't** my classmates. They **are not / they aren't** happy. He **isn't** tall. – He's **not** tall. **I'm not** glad.
Entscheidungsfragen sind Fragen, auf die man mit „Ja" oder „Nein" antworten kann. Bei solchen Fragen mit dem Verb *be* werden Subjekt und Verb wie im Deutschen einfach getauscht: **Aussagesatz** / **Entscheidungsfrage** ***Ich bin** spät.* / ***Bin ich** spät?* ***I am** late.* / ***Am I** late?*	Am I late? Are you twelve or thirteen? Is he / she / it angry? Are they brothers?
Auf Entscheidungsfragen antwortet man im Englischen mit **Kurzantworten**. Für Engländer klingt ein einfaches "*yes*" oder "*no*" unhöflich. *Aufgepasst:* Bei den bejahten Kurzantworten gibt es keine Kurzformen!	Are you angry? – **Yes, I am. / No, I'm not.** Is he going to school today? – **Yes, he is. / No, he isn't.** Are you coming to the party? – **Yes, we are. / No, we aren't.**
In **Befehlsformen** steht *be* oder *don't be* am Anfang des Satzes.	Be quiet. Don't be angry.

ÜBUNG 4 **Ergänze die fehlenden Kurz- und Langformen in der Tabelle.**

bejahter Aussagesatz		verneinter Aussagesatz	
Langform	**Kurzform**	**Langform**	**Kurzform**
I am		we are not	
	they're		you aren't
	he's	she is not	
you are		I am not	
it is			they aren't

ÜBUNG 5 **Bilde eine Frage zu dem Aussagesatz und gib die vorgegebene Kurzantwort.**

Sue is 13 years old. (no)

Is Sue 13 years old? – No, she isn't.

The dog is very old. (yes)

Adam and Sarah are late for class. (no)

We are in the same class. (no)

Tom is our English teacher's son. (yes)

ÜBUNG 6 **Verneine die folgenden Aussagen. Schreibe die Kurzform auf.**

Giraffes are small animals.

My teacher is called Ms Bean.

I am from London.

Joe and Lisa are good at sports.

ÜBEN

ÜBUNG 7 **Deine Klasse macht einen Briefaustausch mit einer englischen Klasse. Hier ist der erste Brief aus England an dich. Füge die fehlenden Formen des Verbs be ein.**

Dear penfriend,

My name ______ Richard. I ______ from England. I live in a small village called Oakham. I ______ 12 years old. My eyes ______ bright blue and my hair ______ brown. I have two sisters. They ______ 13 and 15 years old. My father ______ a teacher and my mother ______ a doctor. They ______ both 40 years old. My favourite hobby ______ music. I ______ the singer in a rock band. I think we ______ quite good. I can send you a tape if *(falls)* you like.

What ______ your hobbies? What do you look like? What ______ your family like? Hope to hear from you soon!

Yours, Richard

ÜBUNG 8 **Verfasse nun einen Antwortbrief an Richard. Nenne deinen Namen, woher du kommst, wie alt du bist, welche Augen- und Haarfarbe du hast. Erzähle von deiner Familie, deinen Hobbys und vielleicht von deinen Haustieren, falls du welche besitzt. Halte dich an den Brief aus Übung 7.**

Dear Richard,

______

______

______

______

______

______

______

Hope to hear from you soon!

Yours, ______

3.3 Das Vollverb *have got*

Das Vollverb *have got* bedeutet *haben, besitzen*. In der dritten Person Singular in der Gegenwart steht *has got*, bei allen anderen Personen *have got*.
Auch hier gibt es Lang- und Kurzformen:

Langform	**Kurzform**
I ***have got***	I'***ve got***
he ***has got***	*he*'***s got***

I **have / I've got** a cat.
You **have / You've got** long hair.
He **has got / he's got** a cool computer game.
We **have got / we've got** a lot of money.
You **have got / you've got** nice shoes.
They **have got / they've got** time.

Ein Aussagesatz in der Gegenwart wird verneint, indem ein *not* zwischen *have / has* und *got* eingefügt wird.

Merke: Bei den Kurzformen fällt das *o* von *not* weg.

Langform	**Kurzform**
I ***have not got***	I ***haven't got***
he ***has not got***	*he* ***hasn't got***

I **have not got / I haven't got** a cat.
You **have not got / you haven't got** long hair.
He **has not got / he hasn't got** a new bike.
We **have not got / we haven't got** a lot of money.
You **have not got / you haven't got** a brother.
They **have not got / they haven't got** time.

Bei **Entscheidungsfragen** (↑ Kap. 3.2) werden Subjekt und Verb wie im Deutschen einfach getauscht.

Aussagesatz	**Entscheidungsfrage**
Du hast Zeit.	***Hast du*** Zeit?
You have got *time.*	***Have you got*** *time?*

Have you got some money?
Has she got a cat?
Have we got the keys?
Have they got a nice house?

In den **Kurzantworten** entfällt das *got*.

Aufgepasst: In bejahenden Kurzantworten gibt es *keine* Kurzformen!

Have you got time? – **Yes, I have. / No, I haven't.**

Have you got your rucksacks? – Yes, we have. / No, we haven't.
Have they got tickets for the show? – Yes, they have. / No, they haven't.

ÜBUNG 9 **Beantworte die Fragen, indem du zuerst die Kurzantwort und dann die korrekte Antwort in der Kurzform gibst.**

1. Has Peter got a car?

   No, he hasn't. He's got a bike.

   Has Peter got a red bike?

2. Have the parents got a new house?

   Have the parents got brown hair?

3. Have the sisters got a horse?

   Has the cat got yellow fur *(Fell)*?

ÜBUNG 10 **Bilde eine Frage zu dem Aussagesatz und gib die vorgegebene Kurzantwort.**

The Smiths have got a dog. (yes)

Have the Smiths got a dog? – Yes, they have.

Jimmy has got a new school bag. (no)

London has got an underground called "The Tube". (yes)

We have got the keys. (no)

I have got a nice room. (yes)

Sarah and Tom have got new bikes. (no)

ÜBUNG 11 **Bilde mit den Satzbausteinen aus den Wolken korrekte Sätze.**

Mrs Collins – Kim and Laura, Sammy – Frankfurt and London – London Zoo

big airports – a lot of CDs – a new comic – many elephants – a horse

has got – have got

WISSEN

Das Verb *have* Wie du bereits weißt, benutzt man das Vollverb *have got*, wenn jemand etwas besitzt.	We have got a blue car.
Das Verb *have* gebraucht man jedoch auch in anderen Wendungen. Wenn es eine **Tätigkeit** bezeichnet, steht es nicht in Verbindung mit *got*. Hier findest du eine Liste mit einigen Wendungen, in denen *have* ohne *got* gebraucht wird.	to have a shower / a bath to have breakfast / lunch/dinner to have tea / coffee / milk to have fun / a party to have a break
Die **Fragen** und **Verneinungen** zu diesen Wendungen werden regelmäßig, also mit der Umschreibung des Hilfsverbs *do* (↑ S. 44), gebildet.	Do you have breakfast at eight o'clock? No, I don't have breakfast at eight o'clock. My brother doesn't have breakfast at all.

ÜBUNG 12 Erinnerst du dich noch an Richard aus England (↑ S. 39)? Dieses Mal erzählt er dir in einem Brief von seinem Tagesablauf. Höre dir Track 4 auf der CD an und setze die fehlenden Formen von *have* und *have got* ein.

4

Hi pen pal,

How are you? I'm fine. Let me tell you about my day. I usually get up at eight o'clock. Then I ________ breakfast. I usually ________ a piece of toast and a cup of tea. My sister ________ toast, she ________ muesli with milk.

After breakfast I take the bus to school. School starts at nine o'clock. Tuesdays are my favourite days: We ________ art and German! And we ________ maths! Do you hate maths, too? At eleven o'clock we ________ a 20-minute break and at one o'clock we all ________ lunch together in our big dining hall. On Wednesdays we ________ rugby or hockey, so I can go home early and play with my dog or play computer games.

My sister and I ________ a new computer and a lot of new games. My family usually ________ dinner at seven o'clock. After that I ________ a quick shower and watch a bit of television or read. I usually go to bed at nine o'clock.

Please write back. Hope to hear from you soon!

Yours, Richard

ÜBUNG 13 Übersetze die roten Satzteile in deinem Übungsheft ins Englische. Verwende *have got*, wenn eindeutig „besitzen" gemeint ist.

Hast du montags Basketball?
Peter hat eine neue Uhr.
Ich frühstücke um acht Uhr.
Peter hat zwischen der 3. und 4. Stunde keine Pause.
Meine Schwester duscht immer abends.

ÜBEN

3.4 *do* als Vollverb und Hilfsverb

Das Verb *do* als **Vollverb *(full verb)*** bedeutet *machen, tun* oder *erledigen*. Es kann sowohl im *present progressive* (↑ Kap. 4.2) als auch im *simple present* (↑ Kap. 4.1) stehen.	Please stop talking, I**'m doing** my homework. I always **do** my homework before dinner.
In der dritten Person Singular im *simple present* steht *does*, bei allen anderen Personen *do*.	Sam **does** sports three times a week. Our dog **does** what it wants.
Do kann auch als **Hilfsverb *(auxiliary verb)*** verwendet werden. Bei verneinten Sätzen steht es zwischen Subjekt und *not* + Vollverb in der Grundform.	You do not like Mondays. I do not eat sausages. We / you / they do not drink coke.
Achtung: Das *-s* der dritten Person Singular wird nicht an das Vollverb, sondern an das Hilfsverb angehängt! Aus *do* wird *does*.	He **does** not play basketball. She **does** not like spiders.
Bei den Kurzformen fällt das *o* von *not* weg.	I **don't** play football. She **doesn't** like music.
In **Entscheidungsfragen** (↑ Kap. 3.2) und bei Kurzantworten im *simple present* wird *do* oder *does* als Hilfsverb verwendet.	Do I know you? Yes, you do. / No, you don't. Do you play tennis? Yes, I do. / No, I don't. Do they eat pizza? Yes, they do. No, they don't.
Achtung: Wie in der Verneinung wandert auch hier das *-s* der dritten Person Singular vom Vollverb zum *do*.	**Does** he like chocolate? Yes, he does. No, he **doesn't**.
Aufgepasst: Do kann in einem Satz doppelt vorkommen, einmal als *Hilfsverb* und einmal als Vollverb.	Sometimes Chris **doesn't do** his homework. **Don't do** that!

WISSEN

ÜBUNG 14 **In den folgenden Sätzen wird *to do* als Vollverb benutzt. Setze die richtige Form des Verbs *to do* ein. Vorsicht: Einmal musst du eine Verneinung verwenden.**

My friends ____ sports every day.

Mrs Spencer ____ her shopping on Saturdays.

Bob and Jane ____ their homework straight after lunch.

Andy ____ some housework to help his mum.

Mrs Adams ____ (not) the cooking, Mr Adams ____ the cooking.

I always ____ the washing-up on Sundays.

Our dog ____ a few tricks.

ÜBUNG 15 **Finde anhand der Tabelle heraus, was die einzelnen Personen mögen oder nicht mögen. Ergänze, was du selbst und ein Freund oder eine Freundin von dir mag bzw. nicht mag.**

	☺	☹
Lisa	horses	cats
Mr Anderson	computers	sports
Nick and Matt	hockey	football
I		
My friend		
We both		

Lisa likes horses, but she doesn't like cats.

Mr Anderson ____, but ____.

Nick and Matt ____, but ____.

I ____, but ____.

My friend ____, but ____.

We both ____, but ____.

ÜBUNG 16 **Übersetze die roten Satzteile ins Englische. Hier brauchst du die Verneinung.**

Wir wohnen nicht in Liverpool. Wir wohnen in Manchester.

Sarah macht ihre Hausaufgaben oft nicht.

Er spielt nicht Tennis. Er spielt Klavier.

Meine Eltern schauen abends nicht fern.

Meine Oma geht nicht ins Kino.

WISSEN

Fragen mit Fragewort und die verneinte Befehlsform Fragen mit einem Fragewort werden genauso mit ***do*** oder ***does*** gebildet wie Entscheidungsfragen. Das Fragewort steht jedoch vor ***do*** oder ***does*** am Satzanfang (↑ Kap. 7.1).	**Where do** you live? **When does** Andrew play rugby?
Merke: Fragen mit *who* als Subjekt bilden eine Ausnahme. Hier wird nicht mit *do / does* umschrieben.	**Who cleans** the rabbit's cage?
Die verneinte Befehlsform wird mit ***don't*** und der Grundform des Vollverbs gebildet.	**Don't be** late. (Komm / Kommt nicht zu spät!) **Don't forget** your homework. (Vergiss / Vergesst nicht deine / eure Hausaufgaben.)

ÜBEN

ÜBUNG 17 **Cheeky ist ein frecher Hund und tut alles, was er eigentlich nicht darf. Mr Jones muss ihn ständig ermahnen. Was sagt er zu Cheeky?**

Don't eat my shoe!

ÜBUNG 18 **In eurer Klasse ist ein englischer Austauschlehrer zu Besuch, den ihr ausfragen dürft. Deine Klasse ist sehr neugierig und hat viele Fragen. Hier sind nur seine Antworten zu lesen. Welche Fragen wurden gestellt?**

Where do you live?

I live in Cambridge.

Yes, I do. I have a son and a daughter.

No, they don't. They go to university.

Oh, I like cycling and I go running a lot.

We usually spend *(verbringen)* our holidays in France. We love France.

Because the weather in France is a lot better than in England.

5

ÜBUNG 19 **George möchte im kommenden Schuljahr auf die *Friends' School* gehen. Er hat ein Vorstellungsgespräch bei der Schulleiterin, die ihm einige Fragen stellt. Höre dir Track 5 auf der CD an und vervollständige den Dialog.**

Mrs Moore: "Hello, George. Nice to meet you!"

George: "Hello, Mrs Moore. Nice to meet you, too."

Mrs Moore: "Well, I'd like to ask you a few questions about yourself, George. How old _____ you?"

George: "I _____ twelve years old."

Mrs Moore: "Where _____ you _____ from?

George: "My family _____ in Manchester."

Mrs Moore: " _____ you _____ school?"

George: "Well, school _____ okay. I _____ maths. But my favourite subjects _____ biology and Spanish. _____ I _____ Spanish at your school?"

Mrs Moore: "Yes, you _____. But we also _____ French, Latin and German. _____ you _____ sports?"

George: "Yes, I _____. I _____ sports. Especially football. I _____ in a great football team at my school. My best friend _____ a football with the autographs *(Autogramm)* of all the players from Manchester United!"

Mrs Moore: "Well, you know, our football and hockey teams _____ quite good, too. The teams _____ on Wednesday afternoons. What else _____ you _____ in your free time?"

George: "My brother and I often _____ in front of our computers, but my sister _____ that, so she always _____: " _____ so boring! _____ outside!" And then we usually _____ with our dog outside."

Mrs Moore: "Well, it was nice to talk to you, George, and I _____ to see you next year!"

George: "Thank you, Mrs Moore. Bye-bye."

ÜBEN

Klassenarbeit 1

45 Minuten

AUFGABE 1 **Füge die fehlenden Verbformen in die Aussagesätze und Fragen ein. Verwende die Kurzantworten, wo möglich.**

1. to be: Robert ______ (not) late.
   ______ Robert late? No, he ______.
   The Dixons ______ at home.
   ______ the Dixons at home? Yes, ______.
2. to have got: My grandparents ______ (not) a car.
   ______ your grandparents ______ a car? No, ______.
3. to have: I ______ (not) milk in my tea.
   ______ you ______ milk in your tea? No, ______.

AUFGABE 2 **Fülle den Steckbrief mit Informationen über dich selbst aus. Schreibe vollständige Sätze.**

name: My name ______.
country: I ______.
age: I ______.
hair/eyes: My ______
and my ______.
brothers and sisters: I ______.
hobbies: My ______.
pets: I ______.
favourite singer/band: My ______.
favourite book: My ______.
favourite colour/-s: My ______.
likes (☺): I like ______.
dislikes (☹): I ______

my photo

AUFGABE 3 **Satzpuzzle: Füge die Teile zu einem vollständigen Satz zusammen. Aufgepasst: Achte auf die richtige Personalform und die angegebenen Satzzeichen! Manchmal musst du das Hilfsverb ergänzen.**

My dad / do the washing-up / often.

when / do your homework / you?

He / in the evening / not watch television.

When / go to bed / you?

I / not tired / be.

She / have got / a bike?

Andrew / not / have got / a bike.

AUFGABE 4 **Übersetze die Sätze ins Englische. Verwende, wo möglich, die Kurzformen der Verben. Denke daran, dass die Zeitangaben im Englischen am Ende stehen (↑ S. 88).**

Peter spielt nicht mit seiner Katze.

Wann beginnt die Schule?

Um neun Uhr haben sie eine Pause.

Magst du Schokolade? – Ja.

Vergiss deinen CD-Player nicht!

Ich mache samstags keinen Sport.

Klassenarbeit 2

45 Minuten

AUFGABE 5 **Ergänze den Text mit den richtigen Formen des Hilfsverbs *to be*.**

My name ______ Rebecca McLoyd. I ______ fifteen years old and I ______ a pupil at Hillmorton High School in Christchurch, New Zealand. Christchurch ______ the largest city on New Zealand's southern island.
My family ______ very big. I have got two sisters and a brother. The girls ______ twins. They ______ four years old and really cute. My brother ______ seventeen. He ______ terrible.
My friends ______ Jamie, Matt and Annika. Jamie and Matt ______ from New Zealand, too. Annika ______ from Germany. She ______ an exchange student. We all ______ friends. We have a lot of fun together.

AUFGABE 6 ***Short answers.*** **Beantworte die Fragen.**

Is Rebbecca from Australia? No, ______.
Are the twins 7 years old? No, ______.
Is Annika from Germany? Yes, ______.
Are the twins from Christchurch? Yes, ______.
Is Rebecca a friend of Michael? No, ______.
Is Annika Rebecca's friend? Yes, ______.

AUFGABE 7 **Vervollständige die Sätze mit *to be*, *to have* oder *to have got*.**

______ Rebecca got two sisters? Yes, she ______ two sisters and she ______ a brother, too.
______ Jamie, Rebecca and Matt ______ a friend from Denmark? No, they ______. They ______ a friend from Germany.
______ Matt and Jamie brothers? No, they ______. They ______ friends.

AUFGABE 8 **Was gehört wem? Schreibe vollständige Sätze.**

	computer	pet	bike	mobile phone
Grandma Elizabeth		✓		
Mr King	✓		✓	✓
the twins	✓	✓	✓	✓
Rebecca	✓			✓

Grandma Elizabeth has got a pet, but

Mr King

the twins

Rebecca

AUFGABE 9 **Was machst du in deiner Freizeit, was nicht? Verwende Formulierungen mit dem Hilfsverb *to do*. Schreibe jeweils zwei Sätze.**

What do you do in your free time?

What don't you do in your free time?

4 Zeiten

4.1 Das *simple present*

Für die Gegenwart *(present)* gibt es im Englischen zwei Formen: die Verlaufsform (*present progressive*, ↑ Kap. 4.2) und das **einfache Präsens *(simple present)*.**	*simple present:* I read, you read, he reads, we / you / they read *present progressive:* I am reading, you are reading, he is reading, we / you / they are reading
Das *simple present* entspricht der Grundform (Infinitiv) eines Verbs. *Merke:* In der 3. Person Singular wird immer ein ***-s*** angehängt!	*Grundform:* to read *simple present:* I read, you read, they read Tom play**s** the piano. Lisa like**s** cats. He work**s** in a bank.
Aufgepasst: Manche Wörter ändern in der 3. Person Singular ihre Schreibweise: ■ Endet ein Verb auf einen Zischlaut [ʃ, tʃ, s], wird ***-es*** angehängt. ■ Endet ein Verb mit Konsonant + *y*, wird das *y* zu *i* und *-es* wird angehängt.	 to catch → he catch**es**, to wash → she wash**es**, to finish → he finish**es**, to miss → he miss**es** to fl**y** → he fl**ies**, to hurr**y** → she hurr**ies**, to cr**y** → he cr**ies**
Das *simple present* wird angewendet ■ bei Tatsachen und Gesetzmäßigkeiten, ■ bei gewohnheitsmäßigen oder wiederholten Vorgängen und Handlungen, ■ bei Aufzählungen und kurz andauernden, aufeinanderfolgenden Vorgängen oder Handlungen.	 School starts at 8 o'clock every morning. This shop sells newspapers. I usually have breakfast at seven o'clock. She often goes shopping after school. He shuts the front door, takes the bus and goes to school.
Die folgenden **Signalwörter** erfordern den Gebrauch des *simple present:* *every day / month / year – jeden Tag / jeden Monat / jedes Jahr* *always – immer* *sometimes – manchmal* *usually – gewöhnlich* *often – oft* *never – nie*	 I go to school **every day.** Grandma **usually** goes shopping on Saturdays. Helen **often** plays the piano. It **never** rains in California.

ÜBUNG 1 **Setze die folgenden Grundformen des jeweiligen Verbs in die 1. Person Singular und die 3. Person Singular.**

to drink	I drink, he drinks	to buy	
to carry		to fly	
to miss		to play	
to catch		to come	
to say		to watch	
to listen		to cry	
to take		to arrive	

ÜBUNG 2 **Formuliere ganze Sätze. Nimm dazu jeweils aus jeder Wolke einen Bestandteil. Achtung: Vergiss nicht das *-s* in der 3. Person Singular!**

go to school on Sundays
eat breakfast at 7 o'clock
forget his homework
meet some friends on the bus
take the bus to school

always usually often
never sometimes

I We Peter She He

WISSEN

to go, to do* und *to say

Die Verben *to go* und *to do* haben in der 3. Person Singular eine unregelmäßige Schreibweise. Bei *to do* und *to say* ändert sich die Aussprache: Aus *do* [duː] wird *does* [dʌz], aus *say* [seɪ] wird *says* [sez].

to go → he go**es**
to do → he do**es**
to say → she say**s**

ÜBUNG 3 **Setze die richtige Form in die Lücken.**

Every Friday, Mrs Smith (pick up) (abholen) ______ her daughter Emma from school. Then they (do) ______ the shopping together. They (go) ______ to a big supermarket outside the city. Mrs Smith and Emma always (buy) ______ fruit, milk and eggs. They (go) ______ to the cashier *(Kasse)* and (pay) ______ for their shopping.

In the afternoon, Emma (do) ______ her homework. Then she (call) ______ her friend Mary. And on Friday evenings, Emma often (go) ______ to the cinema with Mary.

After shopping, Mrs Smith usually (go jogging) ______ in the park. Later her husband (prepare) ______ dinner. In the evening, Mr and Mrs Smith often (watch) ______ a TV film together.

WISSEN +

Umschreibungen mit *do* und *does* Willst du im *simple present* eine Frage stellen oder eine Aussage verneinen, musst du eine Umschreibung mit *do* oder *does* verwenden (↑ Kap. 3.4).	When **do** you usually **have** breakfast? **Does** he **play** the guitar?
Wenn eine Aussage verneint wird, gebraucht man die Formen *don't* und *doesn't* (Kurzformen für *do not / does not.)*	I **don't** have breakfast in the mornings. She **doesn't** like apples.

ÜBUNG 4 **Suche dir aus den Kästchen jeweils etwas, was du magst und etwas, was du nicht magst. Schreibe drei vollständige Sätze in dein Übungsheft.**

Beispiel: I like holidays, but I don't like homework.

I like:

my friends – holidays – football – sunshine – Christmas – chocolate – books – pop music

I don't like:

hardrock – Mondays – maths – rain and cold weather – homework – school exams – fish – computer games

ÜBUNG 5 **Und was mag dein Freund oder deine Freundin? Formuliere mit den Wörtern, die in Übung 4 angegeben sind, drei Sätze in der 3. Person Singular.**

Beispiel: He / she likes holidays, but he / she doesn't like homework.

ÜBUNG 6 **Formuliere zu den Antworten die passenden Fragen.**

Hannah / to live / in Michigan ? – Yes, she does.

School / to start / at 6 o'clock / every morning

? – No, it doesn't. School starts at 8 o'clock every morning.

Hannah and her friends / to eat lunch / in the cafeteria.

? – Yes, they do.

She / to play / the violin ? – Yes, she does.

Hannah and her friends / to go shopping / at the weekends / sometimes

? – Yes, they do.

ÜBUNG 7 **Übersetze.**

Laura spielt täglich auf ihrer Geige.

Lilly füttert gerade die Hasen.

Paul macht nicht gerne Hausaufgaben.

Schau! Die Katze jagt den Hund!

Letzten Sommer waren wir in Spanien.

4.2 Das *present progressive*

Die **Verlaufsform *(present progressive)*** wird gebildet, indem man an die Grundform des Verbs *-ing* anhängt. Zusätzlich benötigt man eine Personalform des Hilfsverbs *to be* (↑ Kap. 3.2).	*Grundform:* to read *present progressive*: I **am** go**ing** home. She **is** read**ing** a book. We / you / they **are** talk**ing**.
Aufgepasst: Manche Wörter ändern ihre Schreibweise, wenn *-ing* angehängt wird: ■ Steht ein kurzer Vokal vor dem Endkonsonanten, wird dieser verdoppelt. ■ Bei einem stummen *-e* am Wortende fällt dieses einfach weg. ■ Endet ein Verb auf *-ie*, wird *-y* daraus.	 to swi**m** → swi**mm**ing, to ru**n** → ru**nn**ing, to si**t** → si**tt**ing to driv**e** → driv**ing**, to writ**e** → writ**ing**, to com**e** → com**ing** to d**ie** → d**ying**
Das *present progressive* wird angewendet, wenn eine Handlung gerade jetzt, in diesem Moment stattfindet.	It's ten o'clock: The children are having breakfast.
Die folgenden **Signalwörter** machen das *present progressive* erforderlich: *at this moment – in diesem Moment* *now – jetzt* *just – gerade* *still – (immer) noch* *Look! – Schau!* *Listen! – Hör mal!*	 **At this moment** the taxi is arriving. I'm going to school **now.** It's May, but it's **still** snowing. **Look,** it's raining.
Um im *present progressive* eine Aussage zu **verneinen**, setzt du *not* zwischen das Hilfsverb und die *-ing*-Form.	Liz and Kate **are not watching** TV, they are talking. Rita **is not going** to school, she is going to her friend's house.
Um im *present progressive* eine **Frage** zu stellen, setzt du die Form des Hilfsverbs *to be* direkt vor das Subjekt des Satzes.	The children are having breakfast → Are the children having breakfast? What are the children having?

WISSEN

6

ÜBUNG 8 **Was machen die Personen gerade? Höre dir Track 6 auf der CD an und schreibe die fehlenden *present progressive*-Formen in die Lücke.**

Dad ____________ lunch.

Lilly ____________ her homework.

Bob and Peter ____________ the bike.

Grandma ____________ the carrots.

Grandpa ____________ in the garden.

Laura ____________ the violin.

The neighbour ____________ a book.

Michael ____________ football.

Kim ____________ TV.

Susie the cat ____________ on the sofa.

ÜBUNG 9 **Wortgitter! Finde zehn Verben, die in der *-ing*-Form stehen, und schreibe sie auf die Zeilen.**

X	V	R	S	A	W	A	B	C	D	H	I	J	C	K	Q	T	U	Z
A	H	U	R	R	Y	I	N	G	F	M	N	Q	L	U	V	W	G	H
O	D	S	D	R	F	E	L	M	G	R	S	R	E	A	D	I	N	G
B	T	X	Y	I	Z	A	A	B	M	C	C	T	A	H	R	O	P	I
P	E	D	I	V	K	L	N	X	A	U	V	W	N	I	I	Q	R	J
P	U	T	T	I	N	G	Y	Z	K	S	F	G	I	J	V	M	N	L
C	E	O	A	N	A	B	T	S	I	T	T	I	N	G	I	K	P	Q
Q	O	P	C	G	U	V	E	D	N	H	I	J	G	K	N	L	R	U
R	D	E	F	W	X	B	B	C	G	K	L	M	N	O	G	S	T	K
A	A	V	W	X	B	F	G	Z	H	B	W	R	I	T	I	N	G	I
G	Y	Z	A	S	T	O	P	P	I	N	G	F	A	G	H	L	M	H

____________ ____________

____________ ____________

____________ ____________

____________ ____________

____________ ____________

ÜBUNG 10 **Schreibe vollständige Sätze in der *present progressive*-Form.**

the girls / at the moment / listen to music

right now / for breakfast / cornflakes / Peter / eat

the boys / at the moment / repair / their bikes

Look! / the bus / not / at the bus stop / stop

the cat / still / in front of / sit / the goldfish bowl

the boys / at the moment / football / play / in the garden

WISSEN

Kein *present progressive* nach *can* oder *must!*
Nach modalen Hilfsverben wie *can* oder *must* (↑ Kap. 3.1) steht nie das *present progressive*, sondern immer die Grundform!

Now father **must clean** his car.
Look, I **can run** very fast.

ÜBUNG 11 ***Simple present* oder *present progressive?***

1. It is Monday morning. Sandra Summer usually ______ (to go) to school on weekdays. But today she ______ (to stay) at home because she ______ (to have) a bad headache.
2. Mrs Summer usually ______ (to work) three days a week in a bookstore. This week, however, she ______ (to work) five days because her boss is on holidays. She ______ just ______ (to sell) a book to a woman with a baby.

3. On Wednesdays, Mr Summer often ______ (to play) a football match with his colleagues from work. Today it is Wednesday, and at the moment, his team ______ (to lead) the match by three goals *(Tore)*.
4. Sandra's CD-player is broken. Mr Summer ______ (to repair) it now. Sandra ______ (not / can / help) her dad.
5. Sandra's brother Peter sometimes ______ (to write) a letter to his grandma. Right now, he ______ (to talk) to her on the phone.
6. It is Friday. Sandra ______ (to be) at school. She ______ (to write) a maths test just at the moment. Sandra ______ (to be) tired, but she ______ (not / must / go) home yet *(darf noch nicht)*.
7. Mrs Summer usually ______ (to read) a book on Saturdays. But today she ______ (to watch) TV because it's the Queen's birthday.

ÜBUNG 12 **Setze die jeweils verneinten Formen von *simple present* und *present progressive* in die Lücken ein.**

	verneintes *simple present*	verneintes *present progressive*
he works	he doesn't work	he isn't working
we talk		
they listen		
you run		
she eats		
they sit down		
I come		
we start		
you play		
I swim		
he drives		

4.3 Das *simple past*

Für einen Vorgang oder eine Handlung, die in der Vergangenheit stattfinden, verwendet man die **einfache Vergangenheit *(simple past)***. Von den regelmäßigen Verben wird es gebildet, indem man *-ed* an die Grundform hängt.	*Grundform:* to listen, to play *simple past:* I listen**ed**, she stopp**ed**, we play**ed**, they repair**ed**
Manche Verben haben im *simple past* nicht die Endung *-ed*, sondern werden unregelmäßig gebildet. Diese Formen musst du auswendig lernen.	to go → went to do → did to write → wrote
Aufgepasst: Manche Wörter ändern ihre Schreibung, wenn *-ed* angehängt wird: ▪ Endet ein Verb mit der Kombination Konsonant + *y*, wird das *y* zu *i* und *-ed* wird angehängt. ▪ Ein stummes *-e* am Wortende entfällt. ▪ Folgt auf einen einfachen Vokal ein Konsonant, so wird dieser verdoppelt.	 to hurr**y** → hurr**ied**, to carr**y** → carr**ied** to liv**e** → liv**ed**, to smil**e** → smil**ed** to ro**b** → ro**bb**ed, to pla**n** → pla**nn**ed
Das *simple past* wird verwendet, um eine abgeschlossene Handlung oder einen abgeschlossenen Vorgang zu beschreiben oder um einen bestimmten Zeitpunkt in der Vergangenheit zu benennen.	Last Sunday, we played a family game. Three years ago we went on a trip to England.
Bei folgenden **Signalwörtern** steht immer das *simple past:* *last week / month / year – letzte Woche / letzter Monat / letztes Jahr;* *... ago – vor...;* *yesterday – gestern;* auch Jahreszahlen haben Signalfunktion.	 I wrote a letter to my brother **last week.** I met my aunt three days **ago.** **Yesterday** was Lily's birthday. **In 1969,** the first man walked on the moon.
Bei **verneinten Aussagen** und **Fragen** lauten die *simple past*-Formen *did* und *did not* (Kurzform *didn't*).	I **did not / didn't** go to school yesterday. When **did** you meet him?

ÜBUNG 13 Setze die Verben ins *simple past*.

to play		to live	
to listen		to plan	
to talk		to carry	
to smile		to like	
to hurry		to start	

WISSEN

Die wichtigsten unregelmäßigen englischen Verben

Grundform (Infinitiv)	*simple past*	deutsche Bedeutung
to be	was (Singular) / were (Plural)	sein
to do	did	machen, tun
to break	broke	brechen, kaputt machen
to buy	bought	kaufen
can	could	können
to come	came	kommen
to draw	drew	zeichnen
to drink	drank	trinken
to eat	ate	essen
to fall	fell	fallen
to feel	felt	fühlen
to fight	fought	kämpfen
to find	found	finden
to forget	forgot	vergessen
to get	got	bekommen
to give	gave	geben
to go	went	gehen
to have	had	haben
to hear	heard	hören
to lose	lost	verlieren
to make	made	machen
to meet	met	treffen, begegnen
to say	said	sagen
to see	saw	sehen
to sell	sold	verkaufen
to stand	stood	stehen
to take	took	nehmen
to teach	taught	unterrichten
to think	thought	denken
to write	wrote	schreiben

ÜBUNG 14 **Trage die richtigen Formen des *simple past* in die Lücken ein.**

1 to make
2 to say
3 to become
4 to buy
5 can
6 to forget
7 to give
8 to go
9 to drink
10 to eat

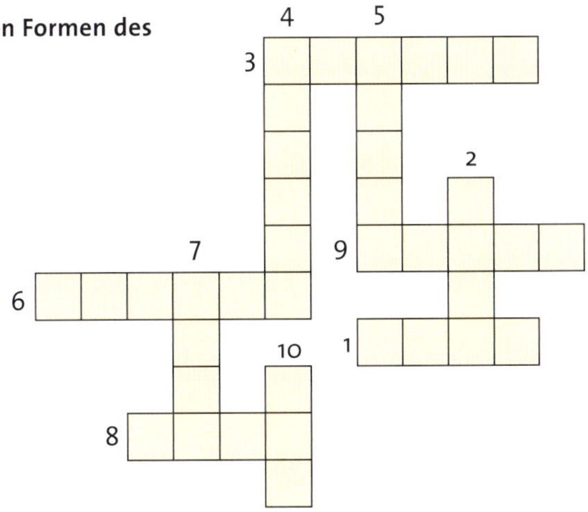

ÜBUNG 15 **Die Geschichte von Aschenputtel (Cinderella). Unterstreiche im Text alle Verben, die im *simple past* stehen.**

Once upon a time *(es war einmal)* there was a man who married *(heiratete)* a woman who already had two daughters. The man also had a daughter. Her name was Cinderella.
Soon after the wedding *(Hochzeit)* everything went wrong. The two daughters of Cinderella's new mother got all the presents, but Cinderella worked all day: she washed the dishes, cleaned the house and made the beds.
But one day, the King's son gave a ball. Cinderella went to the ball and danced with the Prince. The two other daughters were very angry. But Cinderella and the Prince fell in love *(verliebten sich)*, and soon they married and lived happily ever after *(bis ans Ende ihrer Tage)*.

ÜBUNG 16 **Eine Fahrt in die Stadt. Höre dir Track 7 auf der CD an und füge die fehlenden Verben ein.**

7

Yesterday, Liz and her mother ______ into town. They ______ the bus. On their way they ______ a car accident. The police ______ already there. Liz and her mother ______ the bus in front of a big department store. They ______ two T-shirts and a jacket for Liz and a small present for daddy's birthday next week. On their way home, they ______ at a supermarket. They ______ in and ______ potatoes and lettuce for dinner. Then they ______ home and ______ dinner with the whole family.

ÜBEN

Klassenarbeit 1

60 Minuten

AUFGABE 1 **Setze die folgenden Grundformen in die angegebene Form.**

Grundform	3. Person Singular *simple present*	2. Person Plural *present progressive*	1. Person Plural *simple past*
to carry	he carries	you are carrying	we carried
to hurry			
to say			
to listen			
to watch			
to play			
to catch			

AUFGABE 2 **Satzpuzzle – Füge die Satzbausteine zu einem vollständigen Satz zusammen. Achte auf die richtige Zeit: *present progressive*, *simple present* oder *simple past*?**

Yesterday / to be / Michael's birthday

At the moment / to sit / the cat / on the sofa

Look! / to come / the train

Grandma / to visit / last weekend / we

Debbie / to read / at the weekends / a good book / usually

TESTEN

AUFGABE 3 **Wer macht gerade was? Ergänze die Sätze mit den *present progressive*-Formen der Verben.**

run – drive – wait – sleep – dream – feed

The dog ______ for its food.

The mother ______ her baby.

The children ______ home after school.

Grandfather ______ on the sofa.

Our teacher ______ a big car.

We ______ of long holidays.

AUFGABE 4 **Fülle den Lückentext aus.**

Peter (to like) ______ bikes, but he (not / to like) ______ cars.

My mother (to drink) ______ tea, but she (never / drink) ______ coffee.

Liz (to have got) ______ three rabbits and a horse, but she (not / to have got) ______ crocodiles.

Kim (to like) ______ weekends and holidays, but she (not / to like) ______ Mondays.

AUFGABE 5 **Heute ist Freitag, der 13. Ergänze die Sätze.**

Mr Smith usually (to get up) ______ at 7:30 a.m. Now it is 8 o'clock and he (to sleep) ______ still ______.

Maggie often (to play) ______ with her two sisters, but today she is home alone. So now Maggie (to watch) ______ TV.

Nick usually (to do) ______ his homework in his room. But today he can't go home because he lost his key. So he (to do) ______ his homework at school.

Klassenarbeit 2

45 Minuten

AUFGABE 6 **Setze die angegeben Verben in die richtige Zeitform.**

he / sleep *(simple present)*

it / rain *(present progressive)*

you / be *(simple present)*

they / stop *(present progressive)*

she / come *(simple past)*

he / be *(present progressive)*

they / play *(simple past)*

we / swim *(simple present)*

I / read *(present progressive)*

you / drink *(simple past)*

AUFGABE 7 **Ein Vormittag mit Familie Smith: Schreibe vollständige Sätze.**

6 o'clock / Mr and Mrs Smith / get up

7 o'clock / Mr Smith / walk / to the bakery

7 o'clock / Mrs Smith / wake up / Emma and Liz

7:30 / Emma and Liz / get up

8:00 o'clock / the Smiths / have breakfast

8:30 / Mr Smith / go to work

AUFGABE 8 **Auf dem Schulhof: Wer macht gerade was? Ergänze die Sätze mit den Formen der Verben im *present progressive*.**

The children ____________ (to play) football.

Sarah ____________ (to copy) her math homework.

The teachers ____________ (to talk) to each other.

Peter ____________ (to read) a book.

Mary ____________ (to eat) a sandwich.

AUFGABE 9 **Ein kleines Dorf. Unterstreiche das richtige Verb bzw. die richtige Verbform.**

„Little Kingston“ has / does / is a small village.

My grandparents are living / live / lived on a farm there.

The sun shines / is shining / shined today: the horses were / are / are being on the meadow.

The cat sleeps / is sleeping / slept in the sun.

Everyone knows / is knowing / knew each other.

Last week, a circus is giving / gives / gave a show there.

At the moment, grandfather is painting / paints / painted the stable and grandmother cooks / is cooking / cooked dinner.

I like / am liking / liked "Little Kingston".

AUFGABE 10 **Übersetze. Schreibe in dein Übungsheft.**

Mein Vater lebt nicht bei uns.
Jim lädt Mary zu seinem Geburtstag ein.
Maggie steht jeden Tag um 6 Uhr auf.
Ich mag Hunde und Katzen.
Meine Mutter kocht gerade Abendessen.
Peter spielt gerne Fußball.

Klassenarbeit 3

60 Minuten

AUFGABE 11 **Setze die richtige Verbform in die Lücke.**

Every Sunday, the Millers ______ (to get up) late. Then they ______ (to have) a big breakfast. After breakfast, Mr and Mrs Miller usually ______ (to go) outdoors. In summer, they often ______ (to go) biking. In winter, they go ______ (to hike – *wandern*). Their daughter Victoria ______ (not like) biking. After breakfast, she usually ______ (to read) a book. However, her sister Liz ______ (to enjoy) outdoor activities. On weekends, Liz often ______ (to go) climbing. Today is Sunday, but it ______ (to rain) cats and dogs. The Millers ______ (to be) at home. Mr and Mrs Miller ______ (to watch) a DVD, and Victoria ______ (to talk) to a friend over the phone.

AUFGABE 12 **Formuliere zu den Antworten die passenden Fragen.**

Megan / to study / in California

______? – Yes, she does.

The Millers / to go outdoors / every Monday

______? – No, they don't.

They usually go outdoors on Sundays.

Hannah and her friend / to prepare dinner / in the kitchen

______? – Yes, they are.

Lilly / to play / the piano

______

______? – No, she doesn't, she plays the violoncello.

Hannah and her friends / to enjoy / to listen to music together

______? – Yes, they do.

TESTEN

AUFGABE 13 **Das *simple past* – setze die Verbformen in die Lücken ein. Entscheide, ob es sich um eine regelmäßige oder unregelmäßige Verbform handelt.**

Last summer, Lisa and her friend ______ (to spend) two weeks by the seaside. They ______ (to go) swimming every day. They ______ (to get) a good tan *(Hautbräune)*. They ______ (to meet) nice people. They ______ (to eat) ice-cream every day. Every night, they ______ (to have) dinner in a different restaurant. One day, they ______ (to rent – *mieten*) a surfboard and ______ (to try) surfing. They ______ (to have) a lot of fun, but after two weeks the holidays ______ (to be) over. Lisa and her friend ______ (to pack) their suitcases and ______ (to go) home.

AUFGABE 14 **Lies den kurzen Text, ergänze die Lücken und beantworte die Fragen. Benutze dein Übungsheft.**

Last Saturday, an accident happened in Red Lane. Mr Bond wanted to overtake a boy on his bike. Suddenly he saw a big truck in front of him. He tried to brake, but he was driving too fast and crashed his car into a tree. The boy who was cycling was lucky though: he wasn't hit by the car. The truck driver stopped and called the police and an ambulance. Some minutes later the ambulance arrived and took Mr Bond to hospital. A police car arrived at the same time and two policemen took care of the boy. They asked him some questions and then took him home.

What happened (to happen) in Red Lane last Saturday? →

Last Saturday, an accident happened in Red Lane.

Who ______ (to want) to overtake a boy?

What ______ (to see) Mr Bond suddenly?

Why ______ (Mr Bond / crash) into a tree?

Who ______ (to call) the police?

What ______ (to arrive) some minutes later?

TESTEN

AUFGABE 15 **Vervollständige den Dialog. Wende jeweils die richtige Zeit an.**

Lily's mother: "Listen! The phone ______ (to ring). Lily, can you ______ (to answer, *rangehen*) it, please?"

Lily: "This must be Kim ... Hello, Kim! How ______ (to be) you?"

Kim: "I ______ (to be) fine, thank you. Listen, let me tell you a story. Last Sunday, we ______ (to go) to the countryside. My grandparents ______ (to live) on a farm. We often ______ (to visit) grandma and grandpa at the weekends."

Lily: "What ______ you usually ______ (to do) there?"

Kim: "Oh, there ______ (to be) always a lot of work on a farm. Every morning, grandpa ______ (to feed) the horses, for example. And grandma always ______ (to milk) the cows. And I always ______ (to help) them when I ______ (to be) there."

Lily: " ______ your grandparents really ______ (to have) horses, too?"

Kim: "Yes, they ______ (to do). And I usually ______ (to ride) a horse when I ______ (to be) there. But listen, yesterday I ______ (to fall) off the horse and broke my leg. I can't go to school today!"

Lily: "Oh dear! Poor Kim! Listen! I ______ (to come) over right now, okay?"

Kim: "Okay! See you soon, then."

AUFGABE 16 **Übersetze. Schreibe in dein Übungsheft.**

Ich gehe täglich in die Schule.
Mutter kocht gerade das Mittagessen.
Susie mag keine Äpfel.
Schau! Da kommt das Taxi!
Vor drei Jahren waren wir in Australien.
Lily hatte gestern Geburtstag.
Nun muss Betty ihre Hausaufgaben machen.

5 Präpositionen

5.1 Präpositionen der Zeit

Präpositionen der Zeit *(prepositions of time)* geben an, wann etwas geschieht. Am besten lernst du auswendig, wann welche Präposition verwendet wird, auch wenn es einige Grundregeln für ihren Gebrauch gibt.	I have breakfast **at** 7 o'clock. I usually drink some tea **in** the afternoon. My birthday is **on** Sunday 15th October. The classroom is empty **during** the break.
Bei Uhrzeiten und bestimmten Zeitpunkten (z. B. Mahlzeiten und Feiertagen) benutzt man ***at.*** *Aufgepasst:* In vielen Wendungen entfällt hier der bestimmte Artikel, z. B. bei Mahlzeiten und Feiertagen.	at 6 o'clock at the moment at the weekend at Christmas at lunch / at breakfast / at dinner at Easter at night at once
Bei Wochentagen und Datumsangaben (↑ Kap. 8.2) verwendet man ***on.***	on Sunday, on Saturdays, on holiday on Friday 13th, on 22nd March, on my birthday
Bei längeren Zeitabschnitten wie Tageszeiten, Monaten, Jahreszeiten oder Jahreszahlen benutzt man ***in.***	in the morning / in the afternoon / in the evening in December in winter / summer / spring / autumn in 2010 in the past Let's go to the cinema after tea. I always brush my teeth before breakfast. I do my homework between four and six o'clock. Don't talk to your classmates during lessons. The shop is open from 8 o'clock until noon.

ÜBUNG 1 **Welches sind die richtigen Präpositionen? Setze ein.**

um drei Uhr		three o'clock
am Montag		Monday
morgens		the morning
mittwochs		Wednesdays
nachts		night
im Sommer		summer
während des Mittagessens		lunch
am Wochenende		the weekend
am 15. Oktober		15th October
an Ostern		Easter
nach dem Frühstück		breakfast

WISSEN

Orts- und Zeitangaben im ganzen Satz Orts- und Zeitangaben stehen im Englischen meist am Anfang oder am Ende eines Satzes. Im Gegensatz zum Deutschen stehen sie *niemals* zwischen Verb und Objekt.	Ich spiele **sonntags** Fußball. I play football **on Sundays.** **On Sundays** I play football.
Manchmal kommen in einem Satz sowohl eine Zeit- als auch eine Ortsangabe vor. Wenn diese beiden Angaben nach dem Verb (also am Satzende) stehen, wird der *Ort* immer **vor** der Zeit genannt:	My parents go *to church* on Sundays. (*Oder:* On Sundays, my parents go *to church.*) I walk *to school* after breakfast. (*Oder:* After breakfast, I walk *to school.*)

ÜBUNG 2 **Alexander aus Deutschland und Paul aus England sind seit Langem Brieffreunde. Alex will seinen Freund in England besuchen und ruft ihn an, um Genaueres zu vereinbaren. Vervollständige das Telefongespräch, indem du die Präpositionen der Zeit einsetzt.**

Paul: "Hello, this is Paul speaking."
Alex: "Hello, this is Alexander. How are you?"
Paul: "I'm fine, thanks."

Alex: "I talked to my parents. I can come and visit you in England."

Paul: "That's fantastic. When do you want to come?"

Alex: "I don't know. Is it nicer ______ summer or ______ winter?"

Paul: "Hmm, why don't you visit us ______ Christmas?"

Alex: "That's not a good idea. I always spend Christmas with my parents, my grandparents and my brother and sister. Let's meet ______ Easter."

Paul: "Great. We can have a big Easter egg hunt *(Ostereiersuche)* ______ the morning. ______ lunch we usually have a big meal together and ______ the evening we can go to the cinema."

Alex: "That sounds wonderful. Our holidays start ______ Monday 29th March. What's the weather like ______ March?"

Paul: "It can be sunny, but it also rains quite a lot ______ spring. That's our typical English weather."

Alex: "Well, I'm looking forward to *(sich freuen auf)* seeing you ______ 2010."

Paul: "I'm looking forward to seeing you, too. Thanks for your call. Bye-bye."

Alex: "Bye."

ÜBUNG 3 **Schreibe den vollständigen Satz und ergänze dabei die Präposition. Achte darauf, die Orts- und Zeitangaben ans Ende zu stellen.**

have – a big brunch – ______ the weekend – we

____

in the garden – my friend and I – ______ the afternoon – play hockey

____

to school – ______ the morning – I – walk

____

my grandmother – ______ December – I – in London – love to visit

____

and I – ______ autumn– my parents – to Italy – go

____

5.2 Präpositionen des Ortes

Präpositionen des Ortes *(prepositions of place)* geben an, wo etwas geschieht oder wo sich etwas befindet. Sie beschreiben also eine räumliche Beziehung. Meist stehen sie vor Substantiven oder Pronomen.	Lisa is sitting **next to** grandma. Joe is looking for his hamster **behind** the cupboard. Luke lives **near** us.
Es gibt viele verschiedene Präpositionen des Ortes. Auch hier gilt, dass du die wichtigsten Wendungen am besten auswendig lernst. Dies sind die wichtigsten Präpositionen des Ortes:	
in – in	The Woods are sitting **in** their living-room. Caroline arrived **in** Paris yesterday.
on – auf	The butter is not **in** the fridge, it's **on** the table. Please open your books **on** page 11.
under – unter	Is there a monster **under** my bed?
behind – hinter	My little sister is hiding **behind** the sofa.
next to – neben	My father is standing **next to** my mother.
between – zwischen	Can I put the poster **between** the cupboard and the door?
above – über	She is putting the photo **above** her desk.
near – in der Nähe von	Do you live **near** London?
opposite – gegenüber von	The post office is **opposite** the bank.
in front of – vor	I am standing **in front of** the old bakery.

ÜBUNG 4 **Lies dir die Anweisungen durch und zeichne die Gegenstände an den entsprechenden Stellen im Wohnzimmer ein.**

Draw a ball under the table.
Draw a poster above the cupboard.
Draw a CD on the bookshelf.
Draw a ball behind a chair.
Draw a book on the television.
Draw flowers behind the sofa.
Draw a bone in front of the dog.
Draw a schoolbag next to the cupboard.
Draw a pair of shoes under the television.

ÜBUNG 5 **Höre dir Track 8 auf der CD an und füge die fehlenden Präpositionen des Ortes in den Dialog ein.**

8

Tim: "Mum, I can't find it. I looked everywhere _____ my room and it's not _____ the kitchen, either. It's not _____ the shelves and not _____ the coffee maker. I even looked _____ the fridge."

Mum: "What are you looking for?"

Tim: "My mobile phone. Maybe it's stolen *(gestohlen)*."

Mum: "Don't be silly! You often lose things, don't you? I think I saw it somewhere _____ the living-room, _____ the television or on the table _____ the TV guide and my new book. I have an idea! I'll call you on your mobile phone and then we will know where it is."

Tim: "Ah, there it is! I left it _____ the mirror in the hall! Thanks, mum!"

ÜBUNG 6 **Heute hat Kate ihr Zimmer aufgeräumt. Davor sah es jedoch ganz anders aus. Schreibe in dein Übumgsheft, was sich verändert hat.**

Beispiel: Now the schoolbag is not under the bed, it's in front of the bed.

Now the pens ...
Now the CDs ...
Now the comics ...
Now the poster ...
Now the clothes ...
Now the teddy ...

5.3 Präpositionen der Richtung

Präpositionen der Richtung *(prepositions of direction)* drücken eine Bewegung aus.	He's coming **out of** the house. We're getting **into** the car.
Dies sind die wichtigsten Präpositionen der Richtung:	
across – über	A mouse is running **across** the street.
after – hinter ... her	A cat is running **after** the mouse.
against – gegen	Don't lean **against** the window.
along – entlang	My parents always go for a walk **along** the river.
down – hinunter	Anne is walking **down** the hill.
from – aus, von	Are you **from** Cambridge? How far is it **from** Cambridge to Oxford?
into – in ... hinein	Do you want to go **into** this shop?
onto – auf	Sometimes our cat jumps **onto** the kitchen table and steals some food.
out of – aus ... heraus	The family is coming **out of** the shopping centre.
over – über	She is climbing **over** the wall.
past – vorbei	Pam and Annie are walking **past** the swimming pool.
round – um ... herum	I can run **round** the house in 30 seconds.
through – durch	My grandparents are walking **through** the garden.
to – nach, zu	A bus driver takes us **to** school every morning. The train **to** Edinburgh leaves at 10.21 a.m.
towards – auf ... zu	They are running **towards** each other.
up – hinauf	Do you want to go **up** this hill?

ÜBUNG 7 **In dem Wortgitter sind zehn Präpositionen der Bewegung versteckt. Finde und markiere sie.**

H	C	Q	Y	W	E	O	G	T
A	G	A	I	N	S	T	O	H
L	U	C	B	N	T	D	N	R
O	V	R	D	L	T	O	T	O
N	D	O	W	N	B	O	O	U
G	X	S	K	J	T	S	D	G
P	A	S	T	N	V	N	A	H
S	Y	R	O	U	N	D	I	D
Z	W	S	B	W	K	X	V	M

ÜBUNG 8 **Vincent fragt nach dem Weg zum Bahnhof. Füge die passenden Präpositionen der Bewegung in den Dialog ein. Dazu musst du den Stadtplan beachten.**

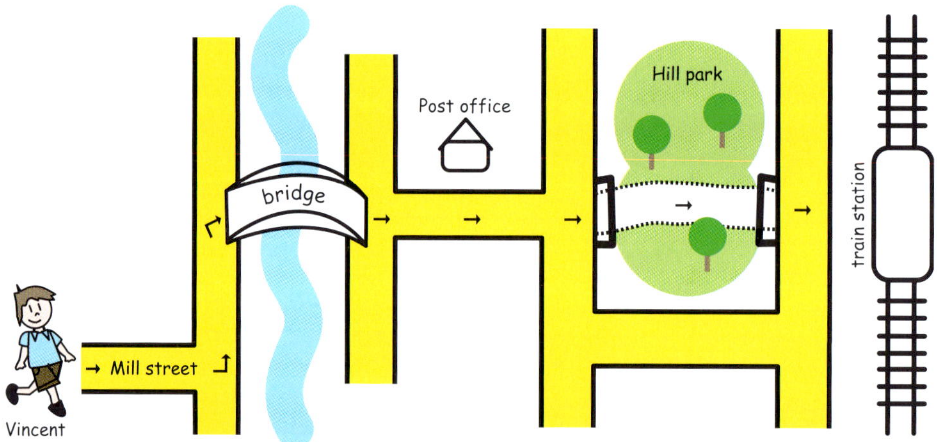

Vincent: "Excuse me, could you please tell me the way to the train station?"

Mr O'Neal: "Oh, that's easy. You just walk d__________ Mill Street until you get __________ the river. At the river you turn left and walk __________ it for 100 yards. Then you walk __________ a bridge and go straight ahead. Walk __________ the post office and i__________ a small park. Go straight __________ the park and as *(wenn)* you come __________ it, you will see the train station."

Vincent: "That sounds very difficult."

Mr O'Neal: "Well, if *(falls)* you get lost, just ask for the way __________ Hill Park."

Vincent: "Okay, thank you very much, Sir. Bye-bye."

ÜBEN

Klassenarbeit 1

45 Minuten

AUFGABE 1 **Zeichne die Bilder entsprechend der Vorgaben.**

1. Draw a ball on a table.
2. Draw a ball under a table.
3. Draw a ball between two tables.
4. Draw a ball next to a table.

AUFGABE 2 **Suche rechts die passenden Zeitangaben in Englisch. Schreibe die fehlende Präposition in das Kästchen. Verbinde anschließend die richtigen englischen Übersetzungen mit den deutschen Angaben.**

an Weihnachten	on	Tuesday
um drei Uhr		Christmas
nachts		winter
am Dienstag		night
im März		three o'clock
im Winter		the morning
zwischen ein und zwei Uhr		March
am Morgen		breakfast
vor dem Abendessen		the weekend
während des Frühstücks		2010
am Wochenende		one and two o'clock
2010		dinner

AUFGABE 3 **Übersetze die roten Satzteile ins Englische.**

Die Katze läuft immer um unser Haus herum.

Nick rannte über die Straße und ins Haus.

Drei Jungs rannten hinter ihm her.

Andy kletterte auf die Garage.

Von dort hat man eine gute Aussicht.

Ben warf Kieselsteine gegen das Fenster.

Kommst du aus Schottland?

Ich fahre nach Edinburgh.

Mr Wilson stieg aus dem Auto.

Er ging am Bahnhof vorbei und auf die Kirche zu.

Ich kann leider nicht zu eurer Party kommen.

AUFGABE 4 **Übersetze die Beschreibung von Bettys Haus ins Englische.**

Mein Zimmer ist über der Küche.

Janes Zimmer ist neben dem Wohnzimmer.

Das Badezimmer ist gegenüber von Janes Zimmer.

Unsere Katze Kitty schläft auf dem Sofa oder in ihrem Körbchen *(basket)*.

Vor unserem Haus gibt es *(there is)* einen Garten.

Hinter unserem Haus ist eine Garage.

Wir wohnen in der Nähe der Bücherei *(library)*.

Klassenarbeit 2

45 Minuten

AUFGABE 5 **Ergänze die fehlenden Präpositionen der Richtung.**

against – through – down – around – to (2x) – from – onto

Don't throw things ______ the window.

Are you ______ New Zealand?

My grandparents are walking ______ the garden.

Our dog usually jumps ______ the living room table.

The plane ______ New York leaves Frankfurt at 8 a.m.

I can swim ______ the lake in 30 minutes.

Dad takes his little girl ______ school every morning.

Flo is riding his bike ______ the hill.

AUFGABE 6 **Ordne die Ortsangaben der richtigen Präposition zu! Lege dazu eine entsprechende Tabelle in deinem Übungsheft an.**

the wall – home – a bus – the bus stop – school – page 25 – London – the table – the kitchen – the book cover – the fridge – the right – the doctor's – Mary's room

at	in	on

Fortsetzung der Tabelle im Übungsheft

AUFGABE 7 **Susan räumt auf. Ergänze die richtigen Präpositionen.**

Where's my ruler? Oh, I see. It's ______ my bag, not ______ my pencil case. Mm, but my exercise book is not ______ my bag. Oh, I can see it now. It's still ______ my desk. That's strange. The flowers are not ______ the windowsill, but ______ the cupboard. Well, and where's the cat? Oh, it's hiding ______ the sofa.

AUFGABE 8 **Ergänze aus dem Wortspeicher die Präpositionen.**

opposite - on (3x) - next to (2x) - in front of - in (2x)

My bedroom is nice: I've got plenty posters ______ the wall. My wardrobe is ______ the door. I've got a blue carpet ______ the floor. There is a big bookshelf ______ my bed. There are many books ______ the shelf. My bed is ______ the door.

I've got a large mirror ______ my room, too. ______ the mornings, I often stand ______ it, to comb my hair.

AUFGABE 9 **Ergänze hier die Präpositionen ohne die Hilfe eines Wortspeichers.**

Peter and Mary are friends. They both live ______ Kingston. Mary gets ______ school ______ foot. Peter gets ______ school ______ bus. Mia gets ______ school ______ bike. She always stops ______ traffic lights. Of course, she has lights ______ her bike.

______ school, the children don't go home. They meet ______ the school playground and play volleyball together.

AUFGABE 10 **Übersetze. Schreibe in dein Übungsheft.**

Meine Mutter ist in ihrem Büro.
Uuuh! Da krabbelt etwas an meinem Bein herauf!
Setz dich bitte hin.
Mary ist von ihrem Fahrrad gefallen.
Dein Englischbuch liegt auf dem Küchentisch.

TESTEN

6 Wortstellung

6.1 Bejahte und verneinte Aussagesätze

Im **bejahten Aussagesatz *(positive statement)*** gibt es eine festgelegte Stellung aller Satzteile. Sie lautet: Subjekt – Verb – Objekt (**S** – *V* – O)

Michael *polishes* his shoes.
Susan *drinks* tea.
We *visit* a museum.

Weitere Satzteile werden einfach angehängt:
S – V – O – weitere Satzteile

Michael polishes his shoes in the kitchen.
Susan drinks tea in the afternoon.
We visit a museum near our school.

Im **verneinten Aussagesatz *(negative statement)*** steht vor dem Vollverb ein Hilfsverb und das Wörtchen *not:*
S – (Hilfsverb + *not*) – V – O

Michael does not polish his shoes.

Susan must not (darf nicht) drink tea.

Merke: can + *not* werden zusammengeschrieben: *cannot*.

We cannot visit a museum.

Auch im verneinten Aussagesatz werden weitere Satzteile an das Ende des Satzes gestellt.

She does not drink tea in the afternoon.
Father does not polish his shoes in the dining-room.

Aufgepasst: In der gesprochenen Sprache werden fast immer die Kurzformen verwendet: *don't* und *doesn't* statt *do not* und *does not*, *can't* statt *cannot*.

She **doesn't** live in London.
We **don't** visit a museum.
You **can't** go to school.

Verben mit zwei Objekten

In manchen Sätzen gibt es zwei Objekte: Das **indirekte Objekt** antwortet auf die Frage „wem?", das **direkte Objekt** auf die Frage „wen oder was?"

Aufgepasst: Für die Wortstellung gilt: Zuerst steht das *indirekte*, dann das direkte Objekt.

My	mother	gave	*me*	a book.
			|	|
Meine	Mutter	gab	*mir*	ein Buch.
			↓	↓
			„wem?" indirektes Objekt	„was?" direktes Objekt

Die häufigsten Verben, die zwei Objekte führen können, lauten: *to bring – bringen* *to buy – kaufen* *to give – geben* *to make – machen* *to pay – bezahlen* *to promise – versprechen* *to read – lesen* *to send – schicken* *to show – zeigen* *to take – nehmen* *to tell – erzählen* *to write – schreiben*	Lucy gives her friend a book for her birthday. Father makes us a sandwich. Grandpa promises Michael a mobile phone for Christmas. I send my penfriend an interesting magazine. The girls tell their friends a good story.

Bindewörter

Die Wortstellung S – V – O gilt im Englischen auch für Nebensätze. Das sind Sätze, die durch ein Bindewort (Konjunktion) eingeleitet werden.	
Die wichtigsten Bindewörter lauten: *before – bevor*	I always eat lunch **before** I do my homework.
because – weil	Laura likes English **because** she likes English pop music.
till / until – bis	Andy plays football **until** the sun goes down.
when – wenn	Grandfather works in his garden **when** the sun shines.
Merke: In Nebensätzen, die auf den Hauptsatz folgen, steht kein Komma! Steht allerdings der Nebensatz an erster Stelle und folgt dann der Hauptsatz, *muss* ein Komma stehen!	*Hauptsatz + Nebensatz:* Linda runs to school because she is late. *Nebensatz + Hauptsatz:* Because Linda is late**,** she runs to school.

ÜBUNG 1 Julie hat einen Aufsatz über ihre Familie geschrieben, doch leider sind die Sätze etwas durcheinandergeraten. Hilf Julie, den Aufsatz neu zu schreiben.

Julie - My - is - name - Clark . in - I - Nottingham - live . old - ten years - am - I . works - My father - a big computer company - for - my mother - and - a teacher - is . two sisters - I - have got - , - Liz - Anne - and . My sister Anne - twelve years old - is . only (erst) six months old - My sister Liz - is . a dog - We - , - have got - too . name - His - Frank - is . in March - is - My birthday . the many presents - like - I . we - And - a lot of sweets - eat - on that day

ÜBUNG 2 Verbinde Haupt- und Nebensätze so, dass sie einen Sinn ergeben. Achte, wo nötig, auch auf die Kommasetzung!

Sarah likes to read books	because she has allergies.
Linda writes a letter	until she gets tired.
Sandy gets good marks *(Noten)*	before she goes to the cinema.
When the sun goes down	because she is clever.
Rachel doesn't have a pet	it usually gets dark, too.

ÜBUNG 3 **Sieh dir die Bilder an und bilde verneinte Sätze.**

This is Lily's room

This is Lily's classroom

Lily sleeps in her bed.

Lily does not / doesn't sleep (not / sleep) in the classroom.

Lily does her homework in her room.

She ______ (not / do) her homework in the classroom.

Lily can watch TV in her room.

She ______ (not / can) ______

Lily waters *(gießen)* the flowers in her room every day.

At school, Tom waters the flowers, so *(also)* Lily ______

(not / water) ______

She reads a book in her room every evening.

Lily ______ (not / read) ______

At home, Lily can listen to music.

At school, she ______ (not / can) ______

Lily has got a rug *(Teppich)* in her room.

Lily ______ (not / have) ______

Lily likes her room at home.

But she ______ (not / like) ______

WISSEN

Classroom phrases

Excuse me, I've got a question.	Entschuldigen Sie, ich habe eine Frage.
Can you say that again, please?	Können Sie das bitte wiederholen?
What's "..." in English, please?	Wie heißt bitte „..." auf Englisch?
What does "..." mean, please?	Was bedeutet bitte „..."?
What do we have for homework, please?	Welche Hausaufgaben haben wir bitte auf?
What page are we on, please?	Auf welcher Seite sind wir bitte gerade?
May I answer in German, please?	Darf ich bitte auf Deutsch antworten?
I'm sorry, I don't understand.	Tut mir leid, das verstehe ich nicht.
I'm sorry, I don't know.	Tut mir leid, das weiß ich nicht.
Can you spell "..." , please?	Können Sie bitte „..." buchstabieren?
Can you write "..." on the board, please?	Können Sie „..." bitte an die Tafel schreiben?

ÜBUNG 4 **Wähle aus dem Kasten jeweils ein direktes und ein indirektes Objekt aus und bilde ganze Sätze. Streiche die Wörter durch, die du verwendet hast.**

the lady – a lie – her sick child – an e-mail – me – an expensive coat – ~~a new camera~~ – the way – to the hospital – his class – her little sister – to nursery school (Kindergarten) – her mother – an interesting picture – ~~me~~ – the old lady

Father promises me a new camera for Christmas.

The shop assistant sells ______

The mother takes ______

The teacher shows ______

She takes ______ every morning.

The girl tells ______

Uncle Rudolph sends ______ every month.

The policeman shows ______

6.2 Orts- und Zeitangaben, Häufigkeitsadverbien

Längere Sätze enthalten oft zusätzliche Informationen, etwa über den Ort, wo etwas geschieht, oder den Zeitpunkt.

Paul sings a song **in the bathroom.**
↓ zusätzliche Information („Wo?")

Ortsangaben *(adverbial phrases of place)* antworten auf die Frage „Wo?“ oder „Wohin?“. Sie beschreiben einen Ort oder eine Richtung und stehen **hinter** dem Verb am Ende des Satzes.

Two girls are playing **in the playground.**
Grandpa works **in the garden.**
↓ S ↓ V ↓ Ortsangabe

Antworten auf die Frage „Wann?“ geben einen Zeitpunkt bzw. einen Zeitraum an. Sie werden **Zeitangaben *(adverbial phrases of time)*** genannt und stehen ebenfalls am Ende eines Satzes.

The school bus leaves **at 7:30 a.m.**
Alex reads a book **after dinner.**
↓ S ↓ V ↓ O ↓ Zeitangabe

Zeitangaben, die besonders betont werden, können auch am Satzanfang stehen. Die Wortstellung bleibt jedoch unverändert!

On Mondays she plays the violin.
↓ Zeitangabe ↓ S ↓ V ↓ O

Aufgepasst: **Ort vor Zeit!** Enthält ein Satz mehrere Angaben, wird erst die Ortsangabe, dann die Zeitangabe genannt.

Our teacher travels to England in summer.
↓ „Wohin?" (Ort) ↓ „Wann?“ (Zeit)

Häufigkeitsadverbien *(adverbs of frequency)* geben an, wie oft oder selten etwas geschieht. Sie stehen im Satz unmittelbar **vor** dem Verb. Zu ihnen gehören:

often – oft
sometimes – manchmal
always – immer
never – nie
usually – gewöhnlich

Peter sometimes clears the table.
↓ S ↓ Adverb ↓ V ↓ O

They always play football in the street.
Sam usually watches TV in the evening.
↓ S ↓ Adverb ↓ V ↓ O ↓ Zeit- / Ortsangabe

Merke: Kommen in einem Satz sowohl eine Zeit- oder Ortsangabe als auch ein Häufigkeitsadverb vor, steht das Häufigkeitsadverb zuerst.

WISSEN

ÜBUNG 5 Wortmix. Erkennst du das gesuchte Adverb?

llsyuua vreen lysawa

tnoef mseeosmti

ÜBUNG 6 So ein Unsinn! Ersetze das Häufigkeitsadverb durch eines, das besser passt.

We never eat ice cream in summer.

The pupils often ask their teacher to give them more homework.

We always enjoy school.

Sarah usually goes to school without shoes.

We sometimes get up late at the weekends.

They never play games with their friends.

ÜBUNG 7 Finde den Fehler in der Wortstellung und verbessere den ganzen Satz; höre dir dazu Track 9 auf der CD an.

ACHTUNG FEHLER

9

Always we go swimming on Saturdays.

We eat a lot of ice cream in summer often.

Our English teacher forgets never to give us some homework.

Tina goes to the supermarket on Tuesdays usually.

Anne and Amy visit their mother sometimes together.

Always Mr Hope helps his wife in the evening.

Laura and Hanna meet their friends on Saturday evenings always.

ÜBUNG 8 Finde die Puzzleteile, die zusammengehören, und bilde daraus Sätze in der richtigen Wortstellung.

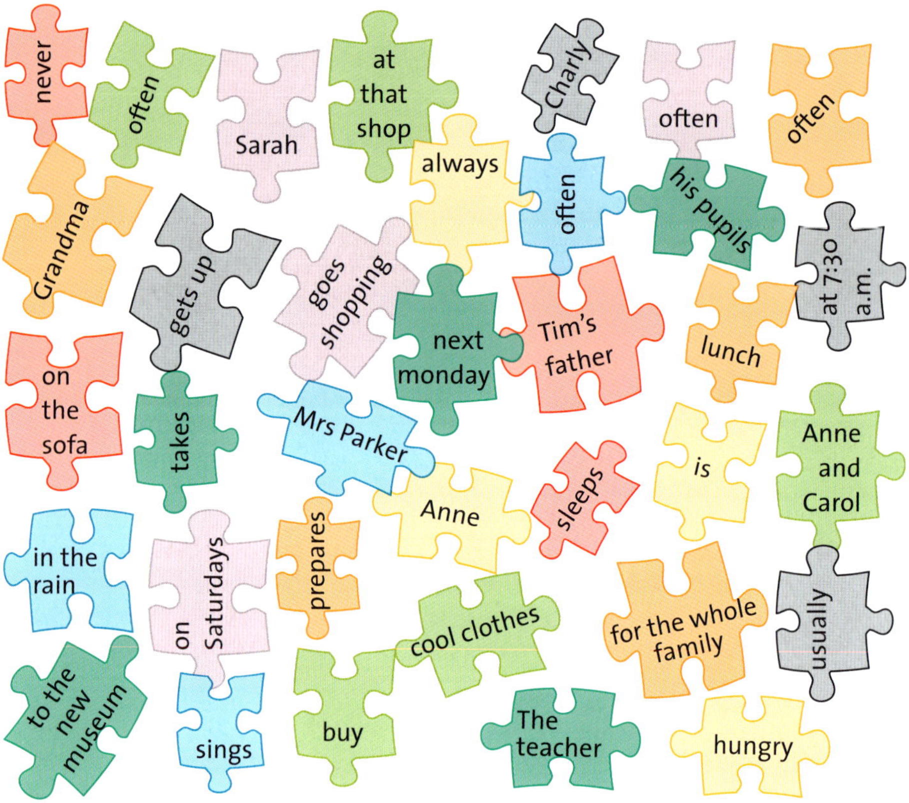

ÜBEN

WISSEN +

Wortstellung bei zwei Orts- oder Zeitangaben Manche Sätze enthalten zwei Ortsangaben. In diesen Fällen gilt für die Wortstellung: Zuerst wird die genauere Angabe genannt, dann folgt die allgemeinere der beiden Angaben.	My teacher travels to Glasgow *in Scotland*. to Glasgow → genauere Ortsangabe (Stadt) *in Scotland* → allgemeinere Ortsangabe (Region)
Für Zeitangaben gilt das Gleiche.	Mandy meets her friend at the youth club at 6 p.m. *on Friday*. at 6 p.m. → genauere Zeitangabe (Stunde) *on Friday* → allgemeinere Zeitangabe (Tag)

ÜBUNG 9 **Bringe die Satzglieder in die richtige Reihenfolge. Schreibe die Lösungssätze in dein Übungsheft.**

Beispiel: at 10 a.m. / always / We / play football / on Saturdays → We always play football at 10 a.m. on Saturdays.

My parents / every day / go to work / at 8 o'clock
travels / Our teacher / to Madrid / in summer / in Spain
Hanna / her homework / at the desk / does / in her room
goes shopping / My mother / in the big shopping centre / every Friday / in town
the school bus / from Monday to Friday / at the bus stop / stops / at 7:15 a.m.
in summer / often / The children / at a big sports centre / go swimming / in town

ÜBUNG 10 **Schreibe die folgenden Sätze in der richtigen Reihenfolge auf.**

The school bus / at 7:30 a.m. / the bus station / leaves

My family / to England / travels / in summer

goes to work / Susie's mum / from Monday till Friday

Carole and Paul / to the cinema / at the weekend / go

My sister Hanna / at the youth club / on Saturdays / meets her friends

6.3 Die Befehlsform

Die **Befehlsform (Imperativ, *imperative*)** ist die Form des Verbs, mit der man einen Befehl, eine Aufforderung, eine Bitte oder einen Vorschlag ausdrückt. Im Englischen entspricht die Befehlsform der Grundform ohne *to*. *Aufgepasst:* Im Englischen steht hinter der Befehlsform normalerweise kein Ausrufezeichen.	Listen. Look. Sleep well. Come here. Hurry up, we are late. Give me my pencil.
Wird eine Befehlsform verneint, werden die Formen ***do not*** oder ***don't*** ohne *to* dem Verb vorangestellt.	Do not lean out of the window. Don't worry. Don't eat all the chocolates. Don't be so lazy!
Merke: Steht *do* vor einer bejahten Befehlsform, erhält die folgende Aufforderung dadurch eine besondere Betonung.	Do sit down, please. Do forgive me, I'm really sorry. Do be quiet!
Aufgepasst: Im Englischen gibt es im Gegensatz zum Deutschen keine Pluralform der Befehlsform. Sie bleibt gleich, egal, ob eine oder mehrere Personen gemeint sind.	Be quiet. ↙ ↘ *Singular:* Sei still! — *Plural:* Seid still! Don't be late. ↙ ↘ *Singular:* Komm nicht zu spät! — *Plural:* Kommt nicht zu spät!
Wenn ein Vorschlag, eine Bitte oder eine Aufforderung auch den Sprecher beinhaltet, verwendet man *let us / let's* + Verb ohne *to*.	Let's go home. (Komm, wir gehen heim.) Let's not get angry. (Wir wollen uns nicht ärgern.)

ÜBUNG 11 **Setze die passenden Befehlsformen ein.**

come – have – help – shut – stop – sleep

_______ your brother with his homework.

_______ in.

_______ the door.

_______ well.

_______ a good time.

_______ this terrible noise.

ÜBUNG 12 **Die Klasse 5a hat einige Klassenregeln aufgestellt. Die Schulstunde reichte aber nur aus, die Bilder zu zeichnen. Hilf den Schülerinnen und Schülern, die Regeln auch als ganze Sätze zu formulieren.**

_______ music in the classroom.

_______ with your classmates.

_______ to your neighbour.

_______ during lessons.

Klassenarbeit 1

45 Minuten

AUFGABE 1 **Setze das richtige Verb in der Befehlsform ein. Achtung: Einmal brauchst du eine verneinte Form!**

open - talk - use - answer - read - look at - take - underline

________ out your books, please. ________ the books on page 32, please. ________ the complete text. ________ a pencil and ________ everything that is important. ________ the questions. ________ pictures in your books, please. And please ________.

AUFGABE 2 **Schreibe die Sätze in der richtigen Wortstellung auf.**

Mr Smith / teaches / English and history / usually

Lily / for breakfast / sometimes / cornflakes / eats

English / learn / at school / Many children

go / We / on Sundays / to the countryside / sometimes

interrupt *(unterbrechen)* / The children / their teacher / never

David and Gordon / at school / on Mondays / usually / play tennis

drinks / two cups of coffee / Mrs Taylor / usually / every morning

do their homework / The children / always / in the afternoon

TESTEN

AUFGABE 3 **Suche aus den Wortspeichern die passenden Ergänzungen für die Sätze unten heraus und vervollständige sie. Achte dabei auf die richtige Wortstellung!**

enjoys / he / because / the countryside	the animals / a lot of food / need / because	is / the weather / when / fine
the cat / but / like / doesn't / it	fresh air / likes / she / because	the sun / till / again / comes out

The Hunts live on a farm. They have a lot of work ______________________ .

Mrs Hunt loves the farm ______________________ .

______________________ the animals are happy.

Their dog loves the farm, too, ______________________ .

Mr Hunt likes his farm ______________________ .

It's raining. Mr Hunt takes the horses into the stable *(Stall)* ______________________ .

AUFGABE 4 **Übersetze. Schreibe in dein Übungsheft.**

Welche Hausaufgaben haben wir bitte auf?
Können Sie bitte das Wort „house“ buchstabieren?
Beeilt euch!
Ich spiele jeden Freitag Tennis.
Unsere Lehrerin fährt jeden Sommer nach England.
Nicht aus dem Fenster lehnen!
Mach dir keine Sorgen!
Sei nicht so faul *(lazy)*!
Kommt, wir feiern am Samstag eine Party!
Können Sie das bitte wiederholen?
Schlaf gut!

Klassenarbeit 2

45 Minuten

AUFGABE 5 **Sortiere die verschiedenen Adverbien bzw. Zeit- und Ortsangaben in die richtige Spalte der Tabelle.**

after lunch – in the playground – never – usually – on weekdays – in the bathroom – often – at home – always – at 7:30 a.m.

Adverbien der Häufigkeit	Zeitangaben	Ortsangaben

AUFGABE 6 **Füge das Häufigkeitsadverb an der richtigen Stelle im Satz ein.**

never: Mary forgets her homework.

always: Laura visits her grandmother on Sundays.

usually: Mrs Cooper goes swimming on Wednesdays.

often: Simon goes biking in the afternoon.

usually: The caretaker locks the school gates at 10 p.m.

sometimes: Bill reads a book.

never: John clears the table.

AUFGABE 7 **Verneine die folgenden Sätze.**

Megan has a lot of homework. → Megan doesn't have a lot of homework.

Peter has a nice bike. →

The twins have a pet spider. →

Lilly shares a room with her sister. →

My grandparents have a big house. →

Stephanie and Shelley have a cool mum. →

AUFGABE 8 **Schreibe die Sätze in der richtigen Satzstellung auf.**

every weekday / Mrs Smith / goes to work / from 8:30 a.m. till noon

in Monrovia, California / Megan and Michelle / go to school

Christy and her children / next Sunday / are going to the cinema / in Los Angeles

last June / to Hawaii / Shelley moved

at the school gates / every morning / the bus arrives / at 8:15 a.m.

AUFGABE 9 **Übersetze. Schreibe in dein Übungsheft.**

Können Sie das bitte wiederholen?
Wir machen normalerweise jeden Sommer Urlaub in Spanien.
Mandy trifft ihre Freundin um 18.00 Uhr am Jugendclub.
Komm her!
Es tut mir leid.
Auf welcher Seite sind wir gerade, bitte?

7 Fragen

7.1 Fragen mit Fragewort

Wenn man sich auf Englisch unterhalten möchte, muss man auch **Fragen *(questions)*** stellen können. Viele Fragen beginnen mit einem **Fragewort**. Die wichtigsten lauten:

who? – wer?	*where? – wo?/wohin?*
when? – wann?	*what? – was?*
why? – warum?	*how? – wie?*
whose? – wessen?	*which? – welche/-r/-s?*

Who likes holidays?
Where are my shoes?
When does school start?
What are you looking for?
Why are you late?
How are you?
Whose pen is this?
Which colour is your hair, blond or brown?

Aufgepasst: who (wer) und *where (wo)* werden von Deutschen häufig verwechselt. Male dir ein Smiley in das *o* von *who* – so bekommt das Wort ein Gesicht und du kannst dir leichter merken, dass es sich bei *who* immer um eine Person handelt!

Wh☺ is your English teacher?

Merke: Die beiden Fragewörter *what* und *which* fragen nach den gleichen Satzgliedern.
What brauchst du, wenn man aus einer unbegrenzten Anzahl wählen kann.
Das Fragewort *which* dagegen verwendest du, wenn die Anzahl an Antworten eingeschränkt ist.

What is your favourite food?
(→ unbegrenzte Anzahl an Möglichkeiten)
Which boy is faster? Alan, Tom or Peter?
(→ nur drei Jungen zur Auswahl)

Wird mit *who* oder *which* nach dem **Subjekt** eines Satzes gefragt, steht das Vollverb nach dem Fragewort. Weitere Satzglieder folgen.

Merke: Das Vollverb steht hier immer in der 3. Person Singular!

Who	likes	chocolate?
Which car	is	faster?
|	|	|
Fragewort (+ Subjekt)	Vollverb	weitere Satzglieder
↓	↓	↓
Who	runs	down the street?

Werden Fragewörter verwendet, um nach dem **Objekt** eines Satzes zu fragen, benötigst du das Hilfsverb *do*.

What **do** the girls tell their friends?
When **does** school start?

Achte auf die Wortstellung! Direkt nach dem Fragewort folgt das Hilfsverb *do*, dann kommt das Subjekt und danach die Grundform des Vollverbs.

I work every day.
→ Why **do** *I work* every day?

Steht das Subjekt in der 3. Person Singular, brauchst du *does!*

He goes to school every morning.
→ Where **does** *he go* every morning?

Merke: Im Aussagesatz vorkommende **Präpositionen** werden im Fragesatz am Satzende wiederholt. Sie können nicht wegfallen!

I'm going to school. – Where are you going **to?**
I work for the Red Cross. – Who do you work **for?**

Willst du eine Frage nach dem Objekt besonders höflich formulieren, verwendest du statt *who* das Wort *whom*.

Who could we ask? → **Whom** could we ask?

Aufgepasst: Beim Formulieren einer Frage wird aus der sprechenden (1.) Person die angesprochene (2.) Person:

I / we → you

I live in Berlin. Where do you live, Philip? (Ich wohne in Berlin. Wo wohnst du, Philip?)
We work every Saturday. Mr Taylor, when do you work? (Wir arbeiten immer samstags. Mr Taylor, wann arbeiten Sie?)

Außerdem können Namen durch das entsprechende Personalpronomen ersetzt werden.

Peter lives in London. → Where does Peter live? = Where does he live?

Willst du dich nach einer genauen Anzahl oder nach einer Menge von Dingen erkundigen, verwendest du die Fragewörter *how much* und *how many*.

- Bei *how many* erwartet man als Antwort eine *konkrete Anzahl.*
- *How much* erfragt *nicht zählbare Dinge*, die man nicht in den Plural setzen kann.

How many pupils are there in your class? – There are twenty pupils in my class.
How much time do you spend in front of the TV screen every day?

Merke: Auch nach dem Preis fragt man mit *how much!*

How much is this dress? – It is £ 70. (Wie viel kostet das Kleid? – Es kostet siebzig Pfund.)

ÜBUNG 1 Finde in dem Buchstabengitter acht englische Fragewörter.

X	F	A	C	A	R	A	W	A	Y	S	T	M	E
A	B	W	C	X	E	W	H	O	S	E	E	F	G
B	W	H	E	R	E	X	H	E	L	P	X	T	I
W	H	E	D	E	A	F	G	I	H	J	W	B	E
B	A	N	A	W	H	Y	X	F	C	K	H	M	N
O	T	P	R	U	O	O	F	I	N	H	O	W	T
B	E	A	R	F	I	N	G	E	R	T	I	P	P

ÜBUNG 2 In diesen Kästchen verstecken sich sechs Fragesätze mit Fragewort. Schreibe sie in dein Übungsheft.

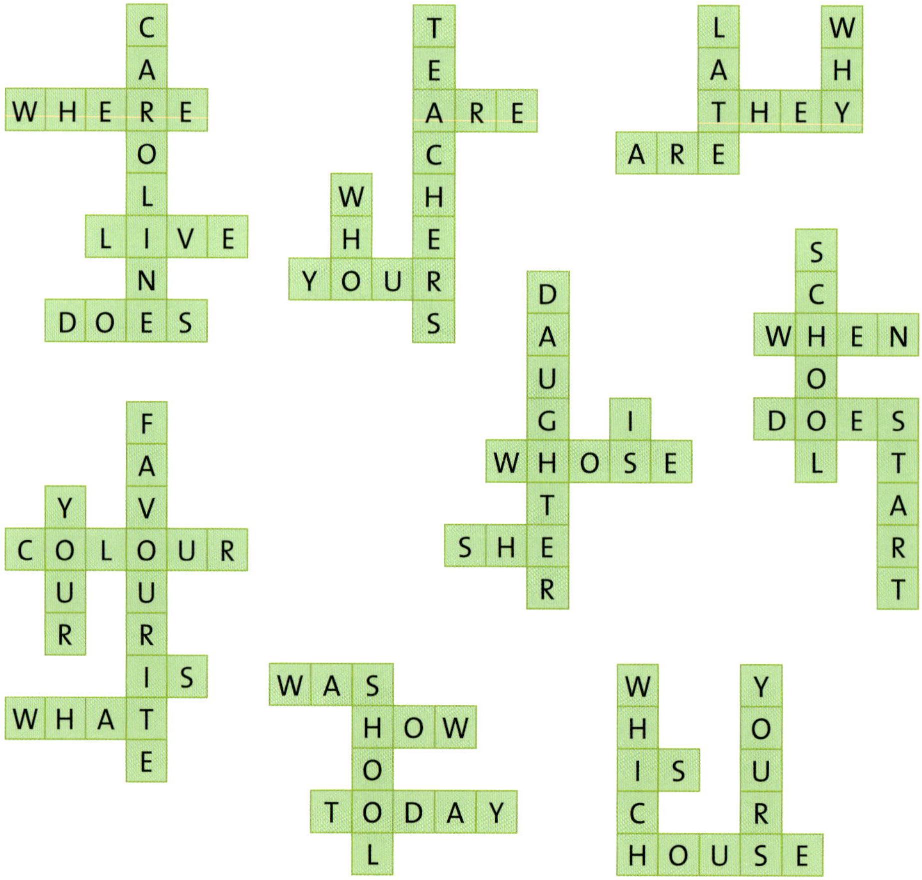

ÜBUNG 3 **Setze die richtigen Fragewörter ein.**

how (1x) – what (2x) – where (2x) – who (1x)

_____ is London? – In Great Britain.

_____ is your name? – My name is Anne.

_____ do you live? – On a farm.

_____ is Mrs Miller? – A maths teacher.

_____ is your favourite colour? – My favourite colour is blue.

_____ old are you? – I'm eleven years old.

ÜBUNG 4 **Setze die richtigen Fragewörter ein.**

Who is? (2x) – Where is / are? (3x) – What is / are? (4x)

_____ Britney Spears? – She is a singer.

_____ mum and dad doing? – They are preparing lunch.

_____ Sydney? – It is in Australia.

_____ dad doing? – He is working in the garden.

_____ Sally doing? – She is doing her homework.

_____ Sally doing her homework? – In the kitchen.

_____ grandma and grandpa going? – To the supermarket.

_____ a tsunami? – It is a very big wave.

_____ Lily? – She is my little sister.

WISSEN

Who is = who's!
Im gesprochenen Englisch wird die Form *is* (3. Person Singular von *be*) häufig verkürzt ausgesprochen: Aus *who is* wird dadurch *who's*.
Merke: Der **Apostroph**, der das weggefallene *i* kennzeichnet, darf auf keinen Fall ausgelassen werden!
Diese Regel gilt auch für die anderen Fragewörter.

Who is this? → Who's this?
Who is your friend? → Who's your friend?

What is your name? → What's your name?
How is your mother? → How's your mother?

ÜBUNG 5 **Stelle Fragen, indem du dich an den rot markierten Wörtern orientierst. Schreibe die Fragen in dein Übungsheft.**

Beispiel: Father watches TV in the living room. →
Who watches TV in the living room?

Laura has a violin lesson on Wednesdays.
Mother reads a book.
The children play basketball in the playground.
Mr Smith owns a supermarket.
We go to the zoo every Sunday.
Most children like chocolate.
Hanna's birthday is in April.
The post office is in Main Street next to the supermarket.
The children like their teacher because she is nice.
The Queen lives in Buckingham Palace.
We all enjoy the holidays.
Mother prepares dinner in the kitchen.

WISSEN

Who's oder whose?

Das Fragewort *whose (wessen)* wird genauso ausgesprochen wie die Kurzform *who's* von *who is (wer ist)*, nämlich [huːz]. Also aufgepasst:

- *who's* erfragt das Subjekt eines Satzes,
- *whose* fragt nach einem Besitz- bzw. Zugehörigkeitsverhältnis.

Who's speaking? = Who is speaking? – Wer spricht?
Whose car is this? – Wessen Auto ist das?
Whose mother is she? – Wessen Mutter ist sie?

ÜBUNG 6 ***Who's* oder *whose*? Formuliere Fragen. Die rot markierten Wörter helfen dir.**

This is Daniel.	Who's this?
Peter is at school.	
Anne and Liz are doing their homework.	
These are Susie's shoes.	
My grandmother is very funny.	
The red house over there is our house.	

ÜBUNG 7 **Lies zuerst die Antworten, schreibe dann die passenden Fragen in dein Übungsheft. Beachte die Wörter in Rot!**

Beispiel: Sarah likes all the Harry Potter films. → Which films does Sarah like?

Fish and chips are Peter's favourite food.
The museum entrance fee is £ 10 for a family ticket.
Bob's car is green.
It's five o'clock.
Peter and Tim both live in Berlin.
There are 15 boys and 13 girls in the classroom.
The post office opens at 8 o'clock.
Our friend feeds the rabbit twice a day *(zweimal am Tag)*.
I want to buy a new computer.
The Smiths and the Patels are our neighbours.
Chocolate is Susie's favourite thing.

ÜBUNG 8 **Stelle Fragen mit *how much* oder *how many*. Schreibe in dein Übungsheft.**

There are five flowers in the garden.
The book is £ 15.
There are seven days in a week.
I have got twenty CDs.
She has got a lot of money in her piggy bank *(Sparschwein)*.

ÜBUNG 9 **Frage nach den unterstrichenen Satzgliedern. Schreibe in dein Übungsheft.**

That's mother's white car over there.
It's midnight.
The apples are 50 pence per pound.
Mother is at work.
Mary has got 15 t-shirts in her wardrobe.
Sam and Lilly are playing football.

ÜBUNG 10 **Höre dir Track 10 auf der CD an und füge die fehlenden Fragewörter ein.**

10

Vicky got £ 20 for her birthday. She wants to buy some toys.

Vicky: "Good morning. __________ are these inliners, please?"

Shop-assistant: "The inliners are £ 15."

Vicky: "Yippeh! So I've got £ 5 left. __________ else can I buy for £ 5?"

Shop-assistant: "Well, the stuffed anmials are £ 4.95 each. __________ is your favourite animal?"

Vicky: "I really love cats. But I've got plenty of stuffed animals. __________ is a computer game?"

Shop-assistant: "Mmm. Computer games are quite expensive. We don't have one that is only £ 5. __________ don't you take a book?"

Vicky: "I usually go to the library. But __________ is that jigsaw puzzle *(Puzzlespiel)* over there?"

Shop-assistant: "That jigsaw puzzle is £ 3.75."

Vicky: "Okay, I'll take that, too."

Shop-assistant: "So that's £ 18.75 all together. Thank you very much."

Vicky: "Bye-bye."

Shop-assistant: "Have fun with your new toys. Bye-bye."

ÜBEN

7.2 Fragen ohne Fragewort

Fragen ohne Fragewort können nur mit *yes* oder *no* beantwortet werden. Sie heißen **Entscheidungsfragen.** Für die Wortstellung gilt immer: **Hilfsverb** – *Subjekt* – Vollverb – weitere Satzglieder	*She* **is** writing a letter. **Is** *she* writing a letter? *You* **can** speak English. **Can** *you* speak English?
Ist kein anderes Hilfsverb vorhanden, wird das **Hilfsverb *do*** verwendet. Die Form von *do* rückt immer an den Satzanfang!	I live in London. → **Do** you live in London? We like red hair. → **Do** you like green hair?
Aufgepasst: Das Hilfsverb *be* lautet in der 3. Person Singular *is*, das Hilfsverb *do* wird in der 3. Person Singular zu *does*.	She **is** beautiful, **isn't** she? **Does** he live in London? – Yes, he **does.**
Bei Entscheidungsfragen reicht ein einfaches *yes* oder *no* im Englischen als Antwort nicht aus. Erwartet werden **Kurzantworten** (↑ Kap. 3.2 / 3.3).	Is she our new teacher? – **Yes, she is.** Has he got a bike? **Yes, he has.**
Eine Frage kann auch formuliert werden, indem man einen Aussagesatz bildet und ein **Frageanhängsel *(question tag)*** anfügt. Diese lassen sich im Deutschen etwa mit *nicht wahr?*, *oder?* wiedergeben.	She is our new teacher, **isn't she?** (Sie ist unsere neue Lehrerin, nicht wahr?)
■ Vollverben bekommen ein Frageanhängsel mit der entsprechenden Form von *do*.	You like chocolate, **don't you?** He runs fast, **doesn't he?**
■ Ist das Vollverb eine Form von *be* oder *have*, wird diese Form von *be* oder *have* wiederholt.	She is our new teacher, **isn't she?** They have got a car, **haven't they?**
■ Bei Hilfsverb + Vollverb wird das Hilfsverb wiederholt.	He can't swim, **can he?** He is going to the cinema, **isn't he?**
Achtung: Das Subjekt des Hauptsatzes wird in der Form des entsprechenden Personalpronomens wiederholt!	Ella lives in London, **doesn't she?**
Merke: Ein bejahter Satz erhält ein verneintes Frageanhängsel, ein verneinter Satz erhält ein bejahtes Frageanhängsel.	Your T-shirt is red, **isn't it?** Dad doesn't like fish, **does he?**

ÜBUNG 11 **Beantworte die Fragen mit einer Kurzantwort. Schreibe die Antworten in dein Übungsheft.**

Beispiel: Is Tilly British? Yes, she is.

	Yes	No
Are you our new teacher?		✓
Is London in Great Britain?	✓	
Is she nice?	✓	
Do you like your birthday present?		✓
Does your mother work?	✓	
Can he swim?	✓	
Do you live in Sydney?		✓
Is Sally doing her homework?		✓
Is the door open?		✓

ÜBUNG 12 **Setze die Hilfsverben als Fragewörter in den richtigen Satz.**

are (2x) – is (1x) – do (3x) – have (2x) – isn't (1x) – can (1x)

	you go to school by bike? – No, I don't.
	your car green? – No, it isn't.
	you from England? – Yes, I am.
	you live in Germany? – No, I don't.
	you got a cat? – Yes, I have.
	mum nice? – Yes, she is.
	you read? – Yes, I can.
	you reading a book? – No, I'm not.
	you got two sisters? – Yes, I have.
	you like school? – No, I don't.

ÜBEN

ÜBUNG 13 Lucy will wissen, was Peter in seinem Schrank hat. Hilf ihr, die Fragen zu stellen!

1. ______________________________ ______________________________?

   "Yes, there are 5 T-Shirts in my wardrobe."

2. ______________________ shoe ______________________________?

   "No, there isn't."

3. ______________________________ ______________________________?

   "There are four towels in my wardrobe."

4. ______________________ dresses ______________________________?

   "No, there aren't."

5. ______________________________ ______________________________?

   "Oh yes! What luck! Thank you so much for finding my maths book!"

7.3 Höfliche Fragen

Die Form ***would like*** wird verwendet, wenn man eine **Frage** sehr höflich formulieren möchte, z. B. um sich nach einem Wunsch zu erkundigen oder um jemandem etwas anzubieten.	What would you like to drink? (Was möchten Sie trinken) Would you like some chocolate? (Möchten Sie etwas Schokolade?)
Möchte man einen **Wunsch** äußern oder jemanden um etwas bitten, kann man mit *would like* auch einen Aussagesatz bilden.	I would like to read a book about New York. (Ich würde gern ein Buch über New York lesen.) I would like a glass of water, please. (Ich hätte bitte gern ein Glas Wasser.) I'd like a cup of tea, please!
Merke: Die Kurzform von *would like* lautet *'d like* und wird in der gesprochenen Sprache sehr häufig verwendet.	
Das Hilfswort ***shall*** *(sollen)* wird verwendet, wenn der Sprecher eine Anweisung erbittet oder jemand ein Angebot machen möchte.	Shall I call the doctor? (Soll ich den Arzt rufen?) Shall I do the shopping for you? (Soll ich für dich einkaufen?)
Auch die Verwendung der Form ***could*** *(könnte)* anstelle von *can* gilt als besonders höflich.	Could you explain the grammar, please? (Könnten Sie mir bitte die Grammatik erklären?)
Im Gespräch werden häufig „unechte" Fragen gestellt. Sie drücken eine Anteilnahme oder ein Interesse aus. Diese ***reply questions*** werden wie die Frageanhängsel (↑ Kap. 7.2) gebildet. Nach einer *reply question* geht die Unterhaltung einfach weiter.	I have got the flu. – **Have you?** Poor girl! (Wirklich? Du Arme!) – Well, I'm already feeling better. My brother likes his friend's sister. – Oh, **does he?** (Ach, tatsächlich?) – Yes, he talks about her all the time.
Aufgepasst: Im Gegensatz zu den Frageanhängseln verlangt eine bejahte Aussage auch eine bejahte *reply question* und verneinte Aussagen eben auch verneinte *reply questions*!	It was a wonderful concert. – Was it? – Yes, it was great! It wasn't a good book. – Wasn't it? That's a pity!

WISSEN

ÜBUNG 14 **Formuliere Fragen oder Wünsche.**

be quiet / for a minute / please / you / would

open / Would / the window / please / you

a sandwich / you / Would / like

next Saturday / you / with me / go/ Would / to the cinema

to the train station / Could / tell us / you / the way / please

a cup of coffee / would / I / like / please

another cup of tea / Would / like / you

WISSEN

Die richtige Begrüßung
Im Englischen gibt es zwei Frageformeln, mit denen man einander begrüßen kann: *How do you do?* und *How are you?* Diese beiden Ausdrücke bedeuten aber nicht dasselbe:

- ***How do you do?*** wird nur dann verwendet, wenn man sich noch nicht kennt, also beim allerersten Zusammentreffen. Die Antwort darauf lautet ebenfalls: *How do you do?*
- ***How are you?*** richtet sich immer an eine Person, der man bereits begegnet ist oder die man gut kennt. Sie erfordert eine ausführlichere Antwort, z. B. *I'm fine, thanks.*

Mr Smith: "Let me introduce ***(vorstellen)*** you: Sarah Miller – Paul Black."
Sarah Miller: "How do you do?"
Paul Black: "How do you do?"

Sam: "Hello Peter, how are you?"
Peter: "I'm fine, thanks. And how are you?"

Klassenarbeit 1

45 Minuten

AUFGABE 1 **Bilde Fragen zu den vorgegebenen Antworten. Benutze Fragewörter.**

? – That is Amy Smith.

? – She's fifteen.

? – She's from Berlin.

? – Her name is Maggie Pole.

? – That's a dog.

AUFGABE 2 **Ergänze die Lücken in den Fragen.**

the next train to London? – It's at 3:44 p.m.

your grandparents? – They are in the garden.

your trousers? – My trousers are blue.

? – It's Luke's.

in bed? – Because she is ill.

? – This book is £ 3.

? – No. Tim is my brother.

? – Thank you, I'm fine.

AUFGABE 3 **Füge die Frageanhängsel ein.**

He is a good boy, ?

You are leaving tomorrow, ?

You have got a lot of money, ?

Pamela looks beautiful, ?

Betty is your sister, ?

Grandmother lives in London, ?

You can swim, ?

AUFGABE 4 **Formuliere Fragen und beantworte sie in deinem Übungsheft.**

Beispiel: Does Peter like chocolate? – Yes, he does.
Does Mary like chocolate? – No, she doesn't.

	Peter		Mary	
	Yes	No	Yes	No
chocolate	✓			✓
biscuits		✓	✓	
homework		✓		✓
holidays	✓		✓	
friends	✓		✓	

AUFGABE 5 ***How much* oder *how many*?**

_______ apples shall I buy?
_______ does a DVD-player cost?
_______ of your friends have got blond hair?
_______ photos shall I take?
_______ of you have got blue shoes?
_______ does your baby weigh *(wiegen)?*

AUFGABE 6 **Übersetze.**

Was ist deine Lieblingsfarbe?
Entschuldigen Sie, wann fährt bitte der nächste Zug nach London?
Möchten Sie einen Apfel?
Wie alt bist du?
Wie heißen Sie?
Mit wem unterhältst du dich?
Wo ist das Schulheft?
Wie viele T-Shirts hat Peter in seinem Schrank?
Wie viel Uhr ist es?
Pinguine *(penguins)* können nicht fliegen, nicht wahr?
Wessen Hemd ist das?

Klassenarbeit 2

45 Minuten

AUFGABE 7 **Finde zu jeder Frage die passende Antwort und verbinde sie mit einer Linie.**

Does Mary have a sister?	Yes, he does.
Do the Miller's have an apartment?	No, I´ve got my own room.
Do you share a room with your sister?	No, she doesn't. She has got two brothers.
Does Steven live in London?	No, they haven't. They've got a house with a garden.

AUFGABE 8 **Formuliere Fragen.**

__________ the train to London? – It is at 10:25 a.m.

__________ ? – No, I´m hungry.

__________ the twins? – They are at the cinema with Grandma.

__________ from Berlin to Frankfurt? – It is about 430 km airline distance.

__________ your bag? – My bag is brown.

__________ yawning *(gähnen)*? – Because she is tired.

__________ ? – Anne is baking a cake.

__________ in the bag? – A folder and three books.

AUFGABE 9 **Formuliere Kurzantworten.**

Is it raining? – No, __________ .

Is Daddy at work? – Yes, __________ .

Can you drive a car? – No, __________ .

Is this a dog? – No, __________ . It's a cat.

Do you like reading? – Yes, __________ .

Are you watching TV? – No, we __________ . We're watching a DVD.

TESTEN

AUFGABE 10 ***Question tags*** **– füge die Frageanhängsel ein.**

She is a good mum, ______ ?

You don't have a lot of money, ______ ?

The dog is naughty, ______ ?

Your aunt lives in New Zealand, ______ ?

They own a big house, ______ ?

Your trousers are blue, ______ ?

AUFGABE 11 **Frage nach den Satzteilen, die unterstrichen sind. Verwende die passenden Fragewörter.**

The bus station is <u>near the school</u>.

My mother gets up <u>at 6 o'clock</u> every morning.

Mary is wearing a cast *(Gipsverband)*, <u>because she has broken her left arm</u>.

<u>Peter's</u> birthday is in January.

<u>Lilly</u> has a music lesson every Wednesday.

<u>The green car</u> is faster than the blue car.

AUFGABE 12 **Übersetze. Achte auf die richtige Verwendung von *How much?* und *How many?* Schreibe in dein Übungsheft.**

Wie teuer ist ein Flug nach New York?
Wie viel Tee soll ich kaufen?
Wie viele Geschwister hast du?
Wie viele Schüler sind in deiner Klasse?
Wie teuer sind diese Äpfel, bitte?

8 Zahlen, Uhrzeit und Datum

8.1 Zahlen

Zahlen *(numbers)* werden in **Grundzahlen** (Kardinalzahlen) und **Ordnungszahlen** (Ordinalzahlen) unterschieden. Mit den Grundzahlen zählt man etwas, die Ordnungszahlen geben eine Reihenfolge an.	*Grundzahlen:* two girls, ten chairs, fifty-six boys *Ordnungszahlen:* the second girl, the tenth chair, the fifty-sixth boy
Zahlen, die aus einer Zehner- und einer Einerzahl zusammengesetzt sind, werden mit einem Bindestrich geschrieben.	twenty-one, thirty-two, forty-three twenty-first, thirty-second, forty-third
Aufgepasst: Im Englischen steht im Gegensatz zum Deutschen die Zehnerzahl **vor** der Einerzahl!	31: einunddreißig, *aber:* thirty-one 45: fünfundvierzig, *aber:* forty-five
Englische Zahlen, die größer sind als 100, erhalten ein *and*.	105 → one hundred and five 2036 → two thousand and thirty-six
Merke: Die Zahlen 100 und 1000 werden *immer* mit dem unbestimmten Artikel *a* oder der Angabe *one* verwendet!	a hundred / one hundred days ([ein-]hundert Tage) – a / one thousand pounds ([ein-]tausend Pfund)
Die ersten drei Ordungszahlen lauten: ***first** (1st)**, second** (2nd)**, third** (3rd).*	the first match – the second year – the third man
Ab der Zahl vier wird an die Grundzahl die Endung ***-th*** gehängt.	the fourth lesson – the tenth pupil – the hundredth car
Aufgepasst: Achte auf die besondere Schreibung bei: *five → fi**f**th (5th)* *eight → eigh**th** (8th)* *nine → ni**n**th (9th)* *twelve → twel**f**th (12th)*	the fifth day of January – the twelfth night
Wenn die Grundzahl auf *-y* endet, lautet die Endung der Ordnungszahl *-ieth.* *twent**y** → twent**ieth** (20th),* *thirt**y** → thirt**ieth** (30th)* usw.	the twentieth day – the sixtieth time

ÜBUNG 1 Verbinde die Zahl mit dem richtigen Zahlwort.

23	thirty-seven	9	eighty-one
37	ninety	3	fifty-seven
42	twenty-three	13	forty
50	a hundred	28	twelve
55	sixty-one	34	thirteen
61	fifty	40	thirty-four
70	eighty-two	57	eighty-seven
82	seventy	12	nine
90	forty-two	81	three
100	fifty-five	87	twenty-eight

ÜBUNG 2 Schreibe die Zahlen aus.

5		49	
15		52	
16		65	
21		79	
25		84	
38		91	
43		100	

ÜBUNG 3 Schreibe die Zahlen aus.

101		620	
243		791	
335		804	
489		910	
552		1000	

ÜBUNG 4 Schreibe die Ordnungszahlen aus.

9th		24th	
50th		32nd	
12th		97th	
1st		20th	
22nd		73rd	
30th		2nd	
88th		11th	
101st		49th	
3rd		52nd	
60th		100th	

ÜBUNG 5 Kannst du das Kreuzworträtsel lösen?

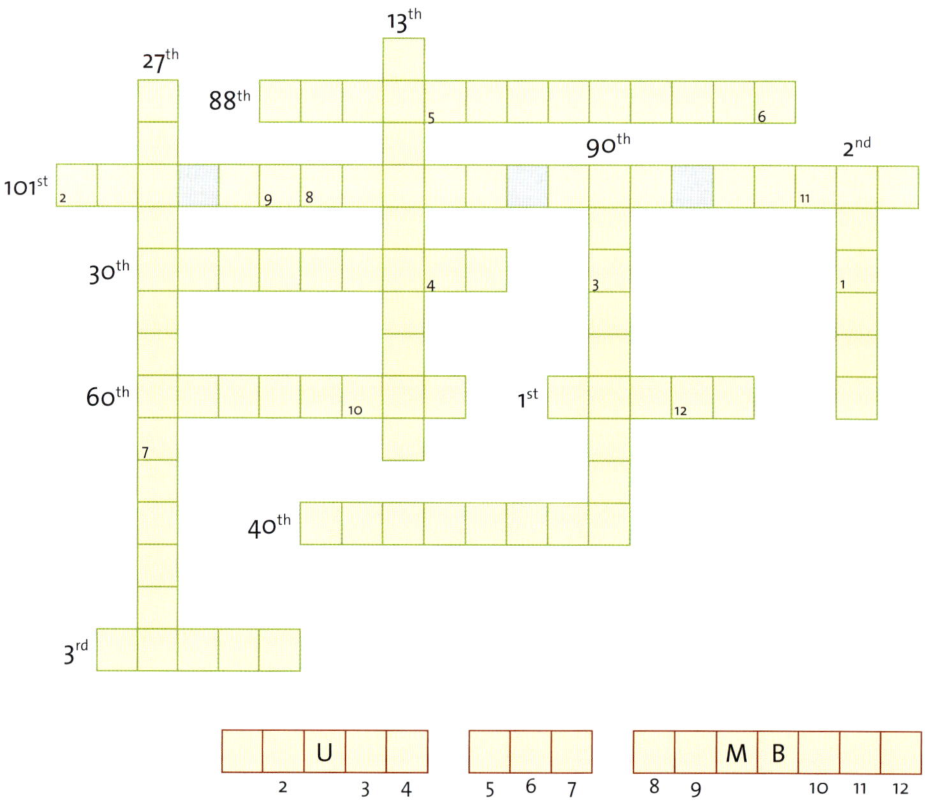

ÜBUNG 6 **Zähle im gleichen Abstand vorwärts oder rückwärts weiter.**

ten, twenty, thirty, ______, seventy

forty-two, forty-four, forty-six, ______, fifty-four

first, second, third, ______, seventh

sixty-five, fifty-five, forty-five, ______, five

seventh, sixth, fifth, ______, first

thirty-two, thirty-one, thirty, ______

______, twenty-six

ÜBUNG 7 **Kannst du gut rechnen? Im ersten Kasten musst du die Zahlen addieren, im zweiten subtrahieren. Als Hilfestellung kannst du die Zahlen in Ziffern in dein Übungsheft schreiben, bevor du das Ergebnis hier einträgst.**

+	seventeen	thirty-three	fifty-nine
seventeen	thirty-four	fifty	
thirty-two			
one hundred and eleven			

–	seven	eighteen	thirty-two
one hundred	ninety-three	eighty-two	
eighty-eight			
sixty-five			

ÜBUNG 8 **Buchstabensalat! Welche Zahl verbirgt sich hinter diesen Buchstaben?**

veneeents = ______

nnnoethounsaadinedtyenin = ______

nvssiyteex = ______

thgeidnahunftyrrddeeeothr = ______

ttenwenniy = ______

11

ÜBUNG 9 **Hier sind ein paar einfache Rechenaufgaben. Höre dir Track 11 auf der CD an und ergänze die fehlenden Zahlen. Rechne anschließend die Aufgaben.**

1\. 1 + ___ = ___
10 + ___ = ___
___ + 4 = ___
___ + ___ = ___
17 + ___ = ___
___ + ___ = ___
___ + 11 = ___
___ + ___ = ___

2\. 10 – ___ = ___
100 – ___ = ___
___ – ___ = ___
___ – 40 = ___
___ – 15 = ___
___ – ___ = ___
20 – ___ = ___
___ – 27 = ___

WISSEN

Die englische Null
In der Mathematik und den Naturwissenschaften heißt die Null *zero*.
In Zahlenreihen, etwa bei Telefonnummern, wird die Null wie der Buchstabe *o* ausgesprochen: [əʊ]. Kommt eine Ziffer zweimal hintereinander vor, sagt man *double* + Ziffer.

Outside it is 10 degrees below zero.
(10 Grad unter Null)

My phone number is 895**0**1**44**.
[eɪt naɪn faɪv əʊ wʌn dʌbl fɔː(r)].

12

ÜBUNG 10 **Verbinde die Lautschrift mit dem dazugehörigen Telefon. Höre dir dazu Track 12 auf der CD an.**

sɪks θriː fɔː(r) faɪv 'dʌbl 'sevn

faɪv tuː naɪn fɔː(r) 'dʌbl wʌn θriː

'sevn naɪn θriː əʊ faɪv sɪks

eɪt tuː 'sevn faɪv əʊ wʌn

8.2 Uhrzeit und Datumsangaben

Uhrzeit *(time)*

Im Englischen wird der Tag in zwei Einheiten zu je zwölf Stunden unterteilt: ■ Die vollen Stunden von Mitternacht bis Mittag werden mit ***a.m.*** (*ante meridiem*, lateinisch für vormittags) bezeichnet. ■ Die vollen Stunden von Mittag bis Mitternacht erhalten den Zusatz ***p.m.*** (lat. *post meridiem*, nachmittags).	1 a.m. – 12 a.m. (1 Uhr nachts bis 12 Uhr mittags) 1 p.m. – 12 p.m. (1 Uhr nachmittags bis 12 Uhr nachts)
Der Zusatz *a.m.* oder *p.m.* entfällt, wenn die Viertel-, die halbe und die Dreiviertelstunde genannt werden: *a quarter past → Viertel nach* *half past → „eine halbe Stunde nach"* *a quarter to → Viertel vor*	It's a quarter past one (Viertel nach eins). The piano lesson begins at half past three (eine halbe Stunde nach drei = halb vier). Now it´s a quarter to eight (Viertel vor acht).
Angaben, die den Zeitraum zwischen der vollen Stunde und der nächsten halben Stunde angeben, werden mit ***past (nach)*** an die letzte Stunde angehängt. Angaben, die den Zeitraum ab der halben Stunde zur nächsten vollen Stunde bezeichnen, werden mit ***to (vor)*** vor die nächste Stunde gesetzt.	It's seventeen minutes **past** two.  It's fourteen minutes **to** five.
Wird die volle Stunde angegeben, so kann man statt *a.m./p.m.* auch ***o'clock*** sagen. *Aufgepasst:* Wird die 12-Stunden-Uhr benutzt, wird die Tageszeit ergänzt, um Missverständnisse zu vermeiden: *in the morning – vormittags* *in the afternoon – nachmittags* *in the evening – abends* *at night – nachts*	It's four **o'clock.** – Es ist 4 Uhr / 16 Uhr. Be quiet. It's three o'clock in the morning (→ 3 Uhr morgens)! I do my homework at seven o'clock in the evening (→ 19 Uhr). The film starts at eleven o'clock at night (→ 23 Uhr).
Aufgepasst: Wenn die Minutenangabe *five, ten, twenty* und *twenty-five* lautet, entfällt das Wort *minutes*!	It's twenty-one minutes past three. *Aber:* It's twenty to two. It's five past six.
Merke: Nach der Uhrzeit fragt man: *What's the time? – Wie spät ist es?* *Can you tell me the time? – Können Sie mir sagen, wie spät es ist?*	What's the time? – It's half past ten. Can you tell me the time? – Yes, it's 3 p.m.

Datumsangaben *(date)*

Das Datum kann man auf unterschiedliche Arten schreiben: Erst den Monat und dann den Tag oder umgekehrt erst den Tag und dann den Monat. Das Jahr steht immer am Schluss, getrennt durch ein Komma.

February 21st, 2010, July 2nd, 1966
Oder:
21st February, 2010, 2nd July, 1966

Merke: Die unterschiedlichen Schreibweisen werden auch verschieden ausgesprochen!

February 21st, 2010 = February the twenty-first, two thousand and ten
21st February, 2010 = the twenty-first of February, two thousand and ten

---

Die englischen **Wochentage** *(days of the week)* heißen:
Monday
Tuesday
Wednesday
Thursday
Friday
Saturday
Sunday

Mother goes to the bakery every Monday and Thursday.

There is no school on Sundays.

Die zwölf **Monate** *(months)* des Jahres lauten:

January	*May*	*September*
February	*June*	*October*
March	*July*	*November*
April	*August*	*December*

My birthday is in January.
Christmas is in December.
In the USA, Independence Day is on July 4th.

Merke: Wochentage und Monate werden im Englischen stets großgeschrieben!

Today is **M**onday, **F**ebruary 15th, 2010.

ÜBUNG 11 **Wie viel Uhr ist es? Schreibe die Uhrzeit in Worten aus.**

1. 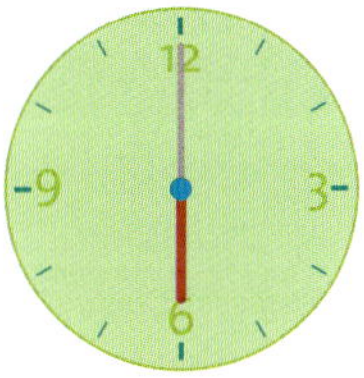

It's

2. 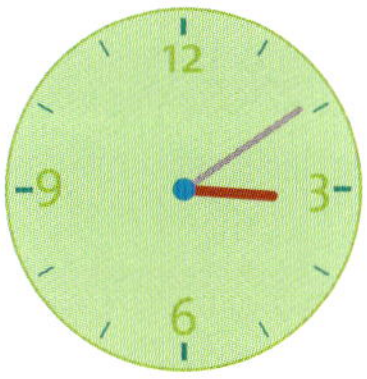

It's

3. 

It's

4. 

It's

5. 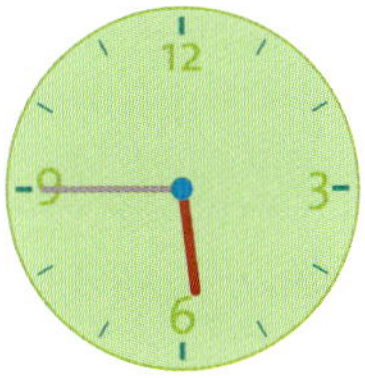

It's

6. 

It's

7. 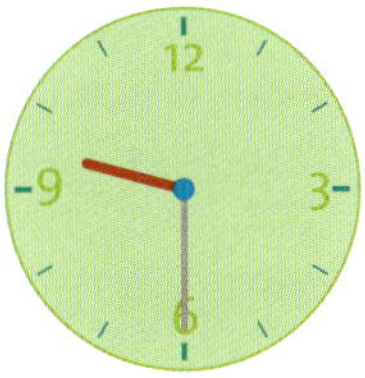

It's

8. 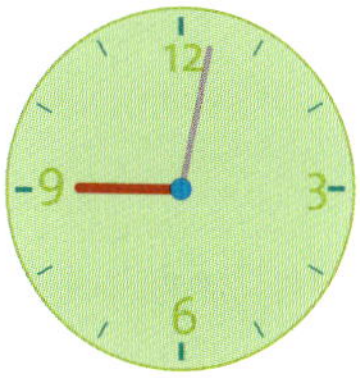

It's

ÜBUNG 12 **Wie spät ist es? Um Missverständnisse zu vermeiden, gib die Uhrzeiten mit der Tageszeit an. Schreibe die Uhrzeiten in dein Übungsheft.**

Beispiel: 4:00 p.m. – It's four o'clock in the afternoon.

5:00 p.m.	9:50 a.m.	11:25 a.m.	6:06 p.m.
6:30 p.m.	10:22 p.m.	12:00 a.m. / p.m.	11:55 a.m.

WISSEN +

Weitere Möglichkeiten, die Uhrzeit anzugeben
Man kann auch die Zeit wie auf einer **Digitaluhr** angezeigt wiedergeben. Nenne einfach die Stunde, dann die Minuten. *Aufgepasst:* Bei dieser Art der Uhrzeitangabe geht die Uhr nicht bis zwölf, sondern bis 24! Die Angabe *a.m.* oder *p.m.* entfällt.

It's 3:17. → It's three seventeen (3 Uhr 17).
It's 15:54. → It's fifteen fifty-four (15 Uhr 54).

Für ***twelve o'clock*** kannst du je nach Tageszeit auch die Begriffe *noon (zwölf Uhr mittags)* und *midnight (Mitternacht)* verwenden.

It's noon. Let's go out for lunch.
We have to catch the midnight train.

ÜBUNG 13 **Die Woche hat sieben Tage. Findest du sie alle?**

A	C	X	Y	T	T	S	R	V	W	S	A	T	U	R	D	A	Y
B	E	E	D	F	U	L	M	N	X	D	I	J	Q	X	T	A	Y
D	G	B	C	W	E	D	N	E	S	D	A	Y	M	N	D	O	M
F	A	E	R	P	S	C	D	F	G	H	I	A	J	N	K	L	R
S	R	O	H	Q	D	X	P	A	P	H	R	H	U	W	M	D	E
L	F	R	I	D	A	Y	D	M	N	O	P	S	I	N	F	G	H
M	N	F	D	G	Y	G	X	K	L	Y	A	E	F	H	I	A	L
A	D	F	D	X	P	H	H	S	D	T	H	U	R	S	D	A	Y
M	N	O	A	E	D	D	P	S	A	Y	F	G	Q	P	S	T	Y
G	M	H	I	M	O	N	D	A	Y	F	L	Q	P	A	B	C	D

ÜBUNG 14 **Ein ganz normaler Schultag. Schau dir Susies Stundenplan an und schreibe ganze Sätze.**

8:05–8:50	maths	10:40–11:25	geography
8:50–9:35	English	11:25–11:35	break
9:35–9:50	break	11:35–12:20	German
9:50–10:35	history	12:20–13:10	French

Susie starts school at five past eight in the morning. She has a maths lesson from five past eight till ten to nine and an English lesson from ten to nine till twenty-five to ten.
Then there's a break from ____ till ____. Susie has a history lesson ____. Then she has a geography lesson ____ ____. There's another *(eine weitere)* break ____ ____ ____. The German lesson is ____ ____. Susie's last lesson, French, is ____ ____ in the afternoon.

ÜBUNG 15 Jeannie hat alle ihre Termine in ihrem Kalender notiert. Heute schreibt sie ihrer Oma einen Brief und berichtet über ihre Woche. Ergänze die Sätze und schreibe die Uhrzeiten aus.

Dear grandma,

Thank you so much for your letter. I am at school all morning from Monday to Friday. On Monday, I take the dog for a walk at five o'clock in in the afternoon / at 5 p.m. .

On Tuesday, I ______ . On Wednesday, I ______ .

On Thursday, I ______ . On Friday, I ______ .

On Saturday, I ______ And on Sunday, I relax!

Love,
Jeannie

Klassenarbeit 1

45 Minuten

AUFGABE 1 **Zeichne die folgenden Uhrzeiten in die Uhren.**

1. It's half past three.
2. It's twenty-five to two.
3. It's a quarter past eight.
4. It's midnight.
5. It's twelve minutes to five.
6. It's half past seven.
7. It's a quarter to six.
8. It's ten to seven.

1. 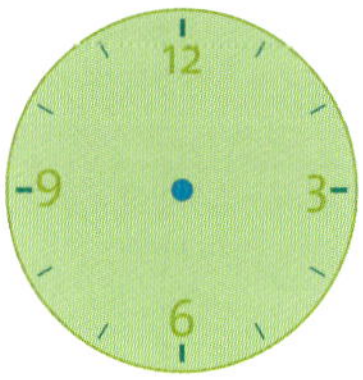

2. 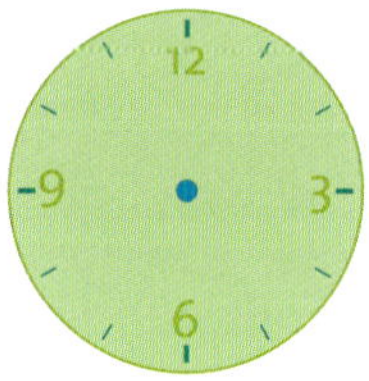

3. 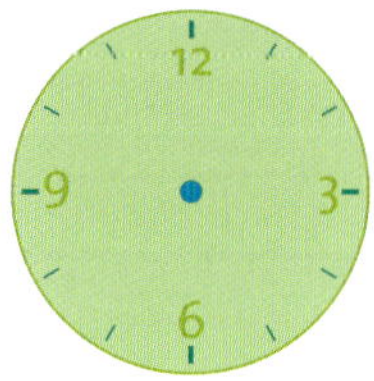

4. 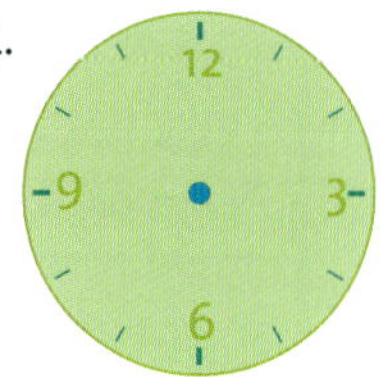

5. 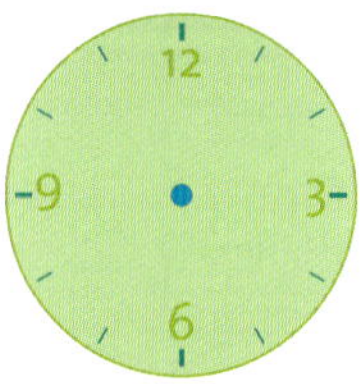

6. 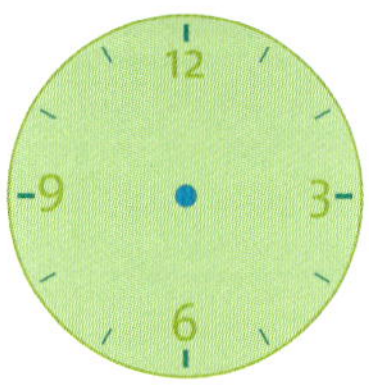

7. 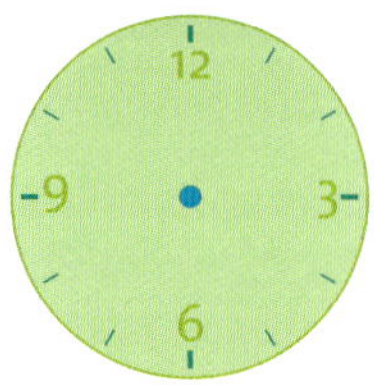

8. 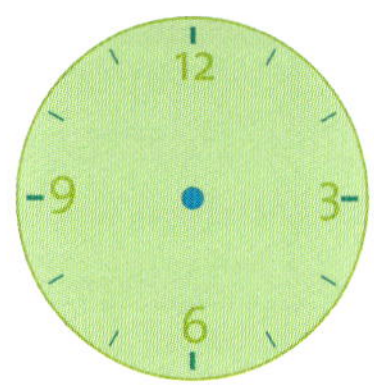

AUFGABE 2 **Schreibe die Uhrzeiten ausführlich auf.**

6:15 a.m.

9:30 a.m.

12:00 a.m. / p.m.

2:26 p.m.

3:48 p.m.

AUFGABE 3 **Beantworte die Fragen. Schreibe nur die Zahl hin, diese aber in Buchstaben.**

How much is 52 plus 26? –

How much is 218 minus 48? –

How many legs does an insect have? –

How many legs does a dog have? –

What date is Christmas Eve? – December

AUFGABE 4 **Tims Englischlehrer sagt die Termine für die Klassenarbeiten an. Schreibe auf, wie der Lehrer die Daten vorliest.**

September 26th ______

December 3rd ______

February 15th ______

1st April ______

10th May ______

24th June ______

AUFGABE 5 **Öffnungszeiten! Schreibe ausführlich auf, von wann bis wann geöffnet ist.**

Dr. Smith
Monday, Tuesday, Thursday, Friday
8 a.m. – 11 a.m.
3 p.m. – 6 p.m.
Wednesday: 9 a.m. – noon

Post Office
Monday – Friday
9 a.m. – 4 p.m.
Saturday
9 a.m. – noon

Michael's Supermarket
open every day from
7 a.m. – 7 p.m.

Maharadsha – Indian Restaurant
open only Saturdays and Sundays
from 11 a.m. till midnight

The post office is open from ______

Dr. Smith's practice ______

Michael's supermarket ______

The Indian restaurant ______

Klassenarbeit 2

45 Minuten

AUFGABE 6 **Suche erst die Grund- und dann die Ordnungszahlen heraus und schreibe sie in deinem Übungsheft aus.**

50th	17	182	2nd	47th
99	1000	72nd	62	31st

AUFGABE 7 **Wie spät ist es? Schreibe die Uhrzeiten ausführlich in dein Übungsheft.**

4:15 p.m.	12:00	3:52 p.m.	11:30 a.m.
8:25 a.m.	7:45 a.m.	4:00 a.m.	9:16 p.m.

AUFGABE 8 **Wie viel Uhr ist es? Schreibe die Uhrzeiten in Worte aus.**

1.

It's

2.

It's

3.

It's

4.

It's

AUFGABE 9 **Hier sind ein paar einfache Rechenaufgaben. Schreibe die Lösungen nicht als Zahl, sondern als ganzen Satz in dein Übungsheft.**

How much is 78 plus 15?
How much is 13 times 5?
How much is 97 minus 83?
How much is 86 minus 24?

AUFGABE 10 **Schreibe die Geburtstage der Familienmitglieder in vollständigen Sätzen in dein Übungsheft.**

Beispiel: Vicky's birthday is on ...

04.01.: Vicky	22.03.: Simon	24.04.: Grandpa Richard
17.05.: Mum	30.10.: Dad	31.12.: Grandma Elizabeth

AUFGABE 11 **Übersetze. Schreibe in dein Übungsheft.**

Der Supermarkt hat von 6 bis 22.00 Uhr geöffnet.
Meine Großeltern essen jeden Tag um 12.00 Uhr zu Mittag.
Das Flugzeug nach New York ist 35 Minuten verspätet.
Der Klavierunterricht beginnt um halb vier.
Wie spät ist es?

Stichwortfinder

DUDEN

Einfach klasse in

Englisch

Lösungsheft

5.

Klasse

1 Substantive und Artikel

ÜBUNG 1 **S. 6**

class → classes, book → books, page → pages, teacher → teachers, pupil → pupils, friend → friends, table → tables, hobby → hobbies, day → days
house → houses, shoe→ shoes, scarf → scarves, cat → cats, bird → birds, dog → dogs, tomato → tomatoes, boy → boys, girl → girls

ÜBUNG 2 **S. 6**

Plural:	Singular:
men	man
knives	knife
children	child
fathers	father
women	woman
feet	foot
posters	poster
teeth	tooth

ÜBUNG 3 **S. 7**

On Peter and Sue's desk are:
two pencil cases
two rulers
three biros
two lunch boxes
two sandwiches
five pencils
two erasers
two pens
two apples
three toys

ÜBUNG 4 **S. 8**

[z] riends
beds
bananas
windows
[ɪz] houses
cages
watches
oranges
[s] books
chocolates
snakes
shops

ÜBUNG 5 **S. 8**

Dear Sarah,
Thank you for your letter. I'm fine. How are you? You wanted to know what I do in my free time? Well, my favourite hobby is hockey. Two **coaches** train our team on Wednesday afternoons. We usually play two **matches** on Saturdays. There are eleven **players** on each team and we all have hockey **sticks**. But there is only one **ball**. Our players wear **green T-shirts** and we all have special **shoes**. A lot of **friends** and **families** come to watch the matches. After the matches we often have dinner together. I usually eat two or three **sandwiches** and drink two small **bottles** of coke. I'm always very hungry after playing. Sometimes my mother brings two big **cakes**. They are yummy!
What are your **hobbies**?
Hope to hear from you soon!
Yours, Andrew

ÜBUNG 6 **S. 10**

Kate: Oh, I'm looking for **a pair of jeans**. What about you?
Sue: I need **two pairs of shorts** for the summer.
Kate: You're right. My old **shorts** are too small. I need a new pair, too. (...) Would you like **a glass of water**?
Sue: No, I think I'll have **a cup of tea**.
Kate: Me, too. Let's get **two cups of tea** at that tea room over there.

ÜBUNG 7 **S. 10**

Your new glasses are nice.
My homework was easy.
Where are my jeans?
I don't have a pair of scissors.
Peter has got two pairs of blue trousers.
My pyjamas are too small.

ÜBUNG 8 **S. 12**
the school's buildings → the schools' buildings
the man's job → the men's job
the girl's room → the girls' room
the child's toys → the children's toys
the woman's hair → the women's hair
the family's cars → the families' cars
the pupil's teacher → the pupils' teacher

ÜBUNG 9 **S. 12**
Julia and Emily's new dog
Lucy's books
the Johnsons' car
the pupils' teacher
Mr Smith's son
the colour of your eyes
the family's TV
the end of the match

ÜBUNG 10 **S. 13**
Mr Rickley's bike – Andy's cake – Lucy's presents – Kate and Sarah's computer – Clare's mobile phone – the girls' pencils – Miss Smith's books

ÜBUNG 11 **S. 15**

an animal	an orange
a fish	a banana
an old cat	an apple
a mouse	an idea
an elephant	an easy exercise
a uniform	a hobby
an uncle	an interesting hobby

ÜBUNG 12 **S. 15**
Dear Andrew,
How are you? I'm fine. Italy is great. **The** weather is fantastic. In the morning we usually have a big breakfast. After breakfast we walk to **the** beach and go for a swim in **the** sea. In the afternoon we sometimes go to little towns by bus. **The** shops are quite nice and **the** clothes are a bit cheaper than in England. We usually sit down in one of **the** cafés and have some ice cream. After supper we often play cards or listen to **the** radio. Sometimes we play table tennis. What are you doing in your holidays?
Love, Sarah

ÜBUNG 13 **S. 16**
Tom: "Hey John, it's your birthday tomorrow, isn't it?"
John: "Yes, it is. I usually have **a** big party. **The** party takes place in our garage because **the** garage is big enough for all of us. Why don't you come, too?"
Tom: "Thanks for **the** invitation. But I'm sorry, I can't come. I have to look after my brother because my mother is at work. She's **a** nurse."
John: "What a shame! It's always great fun. After school most of my friends come to my parents' house in Redwood Road. We usually have **a** yummy birthday cake. Then I open **the** presents and after that we play games."
Tom: "My aunt usually gives me cool things for my birthday. I sometimes get new computer games from her. Do you know what you will get?"
John: "No, I don't. I would love to have **a** new mountain bike. **The** old bike is broken; but mountain bikes are very expensive."
Tom: "Well, good luck! I hope you'll have **a** wonderful birthday party. Maybe I can come over when my mother's back from work."
John: "That's great. See you tomorrow! Bye."

Klassenarbeiten

AUFGABE 1 **S. 17**
man → men
sandwich → sandwiches
baby → babies
boy → boys
woman → women
class → classes
child → children
knife → knives
box → boxes
potato → potatoes
house→ houses
tooth → teeth

AUFGABE 2 **S. 17**

1. I've got two pairs of pyjamas.
I've got three pairs of jeans.
I've got one pair of scissors.
I've got two glasses of water.
2. My trousers are nice.
The glass is empty.
My new glasses are dirty.
The two cups of tea are hot.

AUFGABE 3 **S. 18**

Hi Brad,
We moved into our new house. It is fantastic. Now I have my own little room. My two **brothers** Tim and Joe also have their own rooms. But my two **sisters** share a big room. My **sisters'** room is next to mine and my **parents'** bedroom is also on the first floor.
My **brothers'** rooms are downstairs. **Blacky's** basket is in the hall right next to Tim and **Joe's** rooms, so he doesn't have to sleep in the garage. My **dad's** office and my **mum's** reading room are also on the ground floor. So, now there's enough room for everyone. What's more, the garage is big enough for my **parents'** car, my **brothers'** bikes and the **children's** toys. Come and visit us! We'll have a big party next month. Hope to see you soon.
Yours,
Ben

AUFGABE 4 **S. 18**

Mrs Stevens has got an old car, but Mr Stevens has got a new bike.
The Stevens' new house is at the end of Mill Road.
After breakfast Ben goes to school by bus.
Ben's father is an architect, his mother is a dentist.

AUFGABE 5 **S. 19**

watches; hobbies; buses; lessons; photos; parties; milk; mobile phones; food; fish (fishes); desks; people

AUFGABE 6 **S. 19**

an old house; an English girl; a good book; an hour; a nice party; an attractive teacher; an answer to my question; a young dog

AUFGABE 7 **S. 19**

Mary has got **five pairs of blue jeans** in her wardrobe.
Mary has got **eleven T-shirts** in her wardrobe.
She has got **one hat** in her wardrobe.
Mary has got **two pairs of sunglasses** in her wardrobe.
Mary has got **eight pairs of socks** in her wardrobe.
Mary has got **five dresses** in her wardrobe.
Mary has got **four pyjamas** in her wardrobe.
Mary has got **three pairs of shorts** in her wardrobe.
Mary has got **one swimsuit** in her wardrobe.
Mary has got **two bikinis** in her wardrobe.

AUFGABE 8 **S. 19**

Lösungsvorschlag:
1. pencils; children; houses
2. teachers, pupils, books
3. garden; windows; stairs
4. bike, car, train
5. money, happiness, books

AUFGABE 9 **S. 20**

Make **a** sandwich, please!
May I have **a** cup of tea, please?
Bring **the** milk here, please!
Can you get me **the** phone, please?
Is this **an** empty box?
Now it's your turn, Simon. Throw **the** ball!

AUFGABE 10 **S. 20**

Chocolate Muffins: makes 12–15 medium size muffi**ns**.
You need: 2 eg**gs**, 1 cup sug**ar**, 1 cup flour, 6 teaspo**ons** cocoa powder, 2 teaspo**ons** baking powder, 1 teaspo**on** vanilla essence, 2/3 cu**p** milk, 2/3 cu**p** butter, 4 ounc**es** semisweet chocolate chi**ps**
Preheat oven to 180° C. Grease 12–15 medium muffin ti**ns**. Beat the eg**gs** with sug**ar**, mix with

flou**r**, cocoa powd**er**, baking powder, vanilla and mil**k**. Stir with melted butte**r**. Add chocolate chips and bake for 20 minut**es**.

2 Pronomen

ÜBUNG 1 S. 22

Hi Tim,
I'm going to tell you something about my family. My name is Sue. **I** am eleven years old. My dad is called Adam. **He** is 40 years old. My mother's name is Carole. **She** is 36 years old. **They** are both teachers. **I** have two brothers. **They** are six and eight years old. We live in a very busy street but **we** have a nice garden. **It** is quite big. **We** can play football there. **You** can visit me here. **You** are always welcome.
Lots of love,
Sue

ÜBUNG 2 S. 22

the children → them
Sarah → her
Peter → him
the book → it
our family → us
Peter and Sarah → them
my toy car → it
Mrs Wood → her

ÜBUNG 3 S. 23

Ann: "Hey Kate, there is a new boy in our class. Have you seen **him**?"
Kate: "No, **I** haven't. What is he like? Where is **he** from?"
Ann: "**He** seems very nice. His family moved from Nottingham to London three weeks ago. He's got a sister, too, but I haven't met **her**. **They** live near **us**. Let **us** visit **them**."
Kate: "**I** don't know. I don't know **him**."
Ann: "Don't be silly. He invited **me**. I'm sure **you** can come, too."
Kate: "Okay. Let's go."

ÜBUNG 4 S. 25

his bike – her shoes – their basketball – its saddle

ÜBUNG 5 S. 25

1. Tracy: "Mark, where is **my** schoolbag?"
Mark: "I don't know. There is one over there. Is that **yours**?"
Tracy: "Yes, that's **mine**!"
2. Mark: "Hey Wendy, is this **your** new cat?"
Wendy: "Yes, **it's** cute, isn't it? This is **its** new toy. **It's** a little plastic mouse."
3. Betty: "Andy and Brian are twins. **Their** sisters Hannah and Clare are over there."
Joe: "Are they twins, too?"
Betty: "No, **they're** not."

ÜBUNG 6 S. 26

There are parents with their child.
There is Mrs Burton with her cat.
There is Blacky with his bone.
There are William and George with their bikes.
There is grandpa with his wheelbarrow.
There is grandma with her roses.

ÜBUNG 7 S. 27

Carole is looking for **her** shoes. **Her** brother is helping her. They are looking in **their** bedrooms and in **their** parents' bedroom, but they can't find them anywhere. Carole tells **her** mother: "We're looking for **my** shoes!" – "Ask **your** grandpa. He's in **his** room. Maybe he knows where your shoes are."

ÜBUNG 8 S. 27

they – them – you

ÜBUNG 9 S. 29

this car → these cars
that pet → those pets
that girl → those girls
this boy → these boys
that man → those men
this child→ these children
those bikes → that bike
these chairs → this chair

ÜBUNG 10 **S. 29**
"**This** is my English book here and **that** is your maths book over there."
"Nick, do you like **these** jumpers here better than **those** over there?" – "I don't know, mum, but I like **those** shirts over there."
"Should I buy **this** expensive CD or **these** two cheap cassettes?"

ÜBUNG 11 **S. 30**
Hannah: "Good morning, Mrs Rose."
Mrs Rose: "Good morning, my dear."
Hannah: "Could I have one kilo of potatoes, please?"
Mrs Rose: "Sure. Would you like **these** new potatoes here or **those** sweet potatoes over there?"
Hannah: "**These** new potatoes, please. Are **these** oranges sweet?"
Mrs Rose: "Oh, they're okay. But **those** tangerines over there are lovely."
Hannah: "I'll have six tangerines then, and **that** watermelon next to them. What is **this** round fruit here?"
Mrs Rose: "Oh, **this** is a mango. Try ist! Mangos taste delicious."
Hannah: "Okay, one mango, please. Could I also have a few of **those** bananas over there?"
Mrs Rose: "Of course. Anything else?"
Hannah: "No, thank you very much. That's fine. Bye."
Mrs Rose: "Have a nice day. Bye."

Klassenarbeiten

AUFGABE 1 **S. 31**
Mr Simpson: "Hi Thomas, how was the first day at **your** new school?"
Thomas: "Hi dad, **my** new school is not too bad. My classmates are friendly and **our** classroom is nice, too."
Mr Simpson: "What does it look like?"
Thomas: "Well, **it** is a big room with lots of posters. **Its** windows are also big, so we can look outside when the lessons are boring."
Mr Simpson: "Oh dear. Are **your** new teachers so boring?"
Thomas: "I don't know yet. Our English teacher, Miss Walker, is nice. **Her** two sons are in **my** class as well. **Their** table is next to **mine**."
Mr Simpson: „Well, you must be hungry. **Your** dinner is on the kitchen table."

AUFGABE 2 **S. 31**
siehe unten

AUFGABE 3 **S. 32**
mich → me
sie → them
sie → they
Sie → you
sie → she
mir → me
wir → we
uns → us
unser → our

AUFGABE 2

		Personalpronomen (Subjektform)	Personalpronomen (Objektform)	Possesivbegleiter
Singular	**1. Person**	**I**	**me**	**you**
	2. Person	you	you	your
	3. Person	he / she / it	him / her / it	his / her / its
Plural	**1. Person**	we	us	our
	2. Person	you	you	your
	3. Person	they	them	their

AUFGABE 4 **S. 32**

1. Look, the Millers! **They** are our new neighbours. **Their** house is next to ours. I'm baking a cake for **them**.
2. Lisa: "Peter, is this **your** eraser?" – Peter: "Yes, can **you** give it to me? – Lisa: "Is it really **yours**?"
3. I'm looking for **my** pencil case, but **I** can't find it. Can you help **me**?
4. I found a hedgehog *(Igel)* in the garden. I can show **it** to you, but **it** is very shy. **Its** spines *(Stacheln)* feel strange, don't they?
5. "Who is **that** man over there?" – "I don't know **him**."

AUFGABE 5 **S. 32**

sie → them
unserer → ours
das Bein → his leg
euer Lehrer → your teacher
deiner → yours
ihre Geburtstage → their birthdays
ihren Käse → its cheese
ihre Tasche → her bag

AUFGABE 6 **S. 33**

Anne usually eats cornflakes for breakfast. **She** usually eats cornflakes for breakfast.
Bill has got a red car. **He** has got a red car.
Mr Ledbetter teaches English. **He** teaches English.
My Mum and Dad live in New Zealand. **They** live in New Zealand.
The cat has a broken leg. **It** has a broken leg.
I am a musician. **My** name is Danny.

AUFGABE 7 **S. 33**

Peter is married to Sue. Sue is **his** wife.
Anne and Dave are Peter's children. **They** are brother and sister.
Eve is Anne's sister. **She** has got a brother, too.
Dave is not married, but **he** has a daughter called Amy.
Vicky is Sue's sister. Ron is **her** husband.
Bill and Mary are brother and sister. **They** are cousins of Anne, Dave and Eve.
Eve is married. Harry is **her** husband.
Sue is a grandmother, too. **Her** grandchildren are Amy, Diane and Fred.

AUFGABE 8 **S. 34**

What is **that**? – It's a museum.
Who are **those**? –They are police officers.
Who are **those**? – They are school children wearing a uniform.
What is **that**? – It's Buckingham Palace.
Who are **those**? – They are Beefeaters, guarding the Tower of London.
What is **that**? – It's a bus-stop.

AUFGABE 9 **S. 34**

This is a new car, but **those** over there are very old cars.
This is an English book, but **that** over there is a German youth magazine.
What's **that** building over there?
This cake here is for grandmother's birthday, but **these** muffins here are for you.

AUFGABE 10 **S. 34**

I'll ask my mother for help.
Can you tell me the way to the station, please?
This dog is annoying, but those cats over there are cute.
How tall are you?
Ellen is not at home. She is in hospital.
Our neighbours have got three small children.

3 Verben und Hilfsverben

ÜBUNG 1 **S. 36**

My parents, my brothers an I often **go** the zoo on Sundays. We always **watch** the monkeys and sometimes we **give** them bananas. Afterwards we **walk** over to the penguins. They **are** so cute. At three o'clock the zookeepers **feed** the elephants. They **are** fantastic. I just **love** them. If we don't **go** to the zoo, I usually **stay** at home and **read**. I **like** detective stories and love stories. My brothers **read** lots of comics. I can sometimes **borrow** them.

ÜBUNG 2 **S. 36**
Alex: "No, sorry, I **don't**. **Do** you **need** it?"
John: "Yes, I **must do** my homework."
Alex: "How boring! Why **don't** you **do** it tomorrow?"
John: "I **can't do** it tomorrow because it's mum's birthday. I **need** the book today."
Alex: "You **can have** mine."
John: "Thanks a lot. That**'s** very kind of you."

ÜBUNG 3 **S. 36**
My sister often **plays** with our dog.
I always **do** my homework in the afternoon.
I **like** chocolate.
Some children **hate** school.
Sarah usually **gets up** at 7 o'clock.
School **starts** at 8 o'clock.
Our maths teacher **is** always late.
Sarah **has got** two brothers and one sister.

ÜBUNG 4 **S. 38**
siehe unten

ÜBUNG 5 **S. 38**
Is the dog very old? – Yes, it is.
Are Adam and Sarah late for class? – No, they aren't.
Are we in the same class? – No, we aren't.
Is Tom our English teacher's son? – Yes, he is.

ÜBUNG 6 **S. 38**
Giraffes aren't small animals.
My teacher isn't called Ms Bean.
I'm not from London.
Joe and Lisa aren't good at sports.

ÜBUNG 7 **S. 39**
Dear penfriend,
My name **is** Richard. I **am** from England. I live in a small village called Oakham. I **am** 12 years old. My eyes **are** bright blue and my hair **is** brown. I have two sisters. They **are** 13 and 15 years old. My father **is** a teacher and my mother **is** a doctor. They **are** both 40 years old. My favourite hobby **is** music. I **am** the singer in a rock band. I think we **are** quite good. I can send you a tape if you like.
What **are** your hobbies? What do you look like? What **is** your family like?
Hope to hear from you soon!
Yours, Richard

ÜBUNG 8 **S. 39**
Lösungsvorschlag:
Dear Richard,
My name is Nicole. I am from Germany. I live in Frankfurt. I am 12 years old. My eyes are brown and my hair is blond. I have one brother. He is 15 years old. My father is 40 years old and my mother is 41 years old. My hobbies are horse riding and in-line skating but I also like reading. We have a dog called Blacky. I often go for a walk with him. Have you got any pets?
Hope to hear from you soon!
Yours, Nicole

ÜBUNG 4

bejahter Aussagesatz		**verneinter Aussagesatz**	
Langform	*Kurzform*	*Langform*	*Kurzform*
I am	**I'm**	we are not	**we aren't**
they are	they're	**you are not**	you aren't
he ist	he's	she ist not	**she isn't**
you are	**you're**	I am not	**I'm not**
it is	**it's**	**they are not**	they aren't

ÜBUNG 9 S. 41

1. No, he hasn't. He's got a grey bike.
2. No, they haven't. They've got an old house. – No, they haven't. They've got blond hair.
3. No, they haven't. They've got a cat.
No, it hasn't. It's got black and white fur.

ÜBUNG 10 S. 41

Has Jimmy got a new school bag? – No, he hasn't.
Has London got an underground called "The Tube"? – Yes, it has.
Have we got the keys? – No, we haven't.
Have I got a nice room? – Yes, I have.
Have Sarah and Tom got new bikes? – No, they haven't.

ÜBUNG 11 S. 42

Mrs Collins has got a horse.
Kim and Laura have got a lot of CDs.
Sammy has got a new comic.
Frankfurt and London have got big airports.
London Zoo has got many elephants.

ÜBUNG 12 S. 43

Hi pen pal,
How are you? I'm fine. Let me tell you about my day. I usually get up at eight o'clock. Then I **have** breakfast. I usually **have** a piece of toast and a cup of tea. My sister **doesn't have** toast, she **has** muesli with milk.
After breakfast I take the bus to school. School starts at nine o'clock. Tuesdays are my favourite days: We **have** art and German! And we **don't have** maths! Do you hate maths, too? At eleven o'clock we **have** a 20-minute break and at one o'clock we all **have** lunch together in our big dining hall. On Wednesdays we **don't have** rugby or hockey, so I can go home early and play with my dog or play computer games.
My sister and I **have got** a new computer and a lot of new games. My family usually **has** dinner at seven o'clock. After that I **have** a quick shower and watch a bit of television or read.
I usually go to bed at nine o'clock.
Please write back.
Hope to hear from you soon!
Yours, Richard

ÜBUNG 13 S. 43

Do you have basketball
Peter has got
I have breakfast
Peter doesn't have a break
My sister has a shower

ÜBUNG 14 S. 45

My friends **do** sports every day.
Mrs Spencer **does** her shopping on Saturdays.
Bob and Jane **do** their homework straight after lunch.
Andy **does** some housework to help his mum.
Mrs Adams **doesn't do** the cooking, Mr Adams **does** the cooking.
I always **do** the washing-up on Sundays.
Our dog **does** a few tricks.

ÜBUNG 15 S. 45

Mr Anderson likes computers, but he doesn't like sports.
Nick and Matt like hockey, but they don't like football.
(Beispiel:) I like chocolate, but I don't like ice-cream.
(Beispiel:) My friend Tina likes tennis, but she doesn't like badminton.
(Beispiel:) We both like books, but we don't like homework.

ÜBUNG 16 S. 46

We don't live – We live
Sarah doesn't do
He doesn't play – He plays
My parents don't watch TV
My grandmother doesn't go

ÜBUNG 17 S. 47

Don't bark.
Don't play with my socks.
Don't eat the cat's food.
Don't sleep on the couch.

ÜBUNG 18 **S. 47**

Do you have children?
Do they go to school?
What do you do in your free time?
Where do you spend your holidays?
Why do you love France?

ÜBUNG 19 **S. 48**

Mrs Moore: "Hello, George. Nice to meet you!"
George: "Hello, Mrs Moore. Nice to meet you, too."
Mrs Moore: "Well, I'd like to ask you a few questions about yourself, George. How old **are** you?"
George: "I **am / 'm** twelve years old."
Mrs Moore: "Where **do** you **come** from?
George: "My family **lives** in Manchester."
Mrs Moore: "**Do** you **like** school?"
George: "Well, school **is** okay. I **don't like** maths. But my favourite subjects **are** biology and Spanish. **Can** I **learn** Spanish at your school?"
Mrs Moore: "Yes, you **can**. But we also **teach** French, Latin and German. **Do** you **like** sports?"
George: "Yes, I **do**. I **love** sports. Especially football. I **play** in a great football team at my school. My best friend **has got** a football with the autographs of all the players from Manchester United!"
Mrs Moore: "Well, you know, our football and hockey teams **are** quite good, too. The teams **train** on Wednesday afternoons. What else **do** you **do** in your free time?"
George: "My brother and I often **sit** in front of our computers, but my sister **doesn't like** that, so she always **says**: "**Don't be** so boring! **Come** outside!" And then we usually **play** with our dog outside."
Mrs Moore: "Well, it was nice to talk to you, George, and I **hope** to see you next year!"
George: "Thank you, Mrs Moore. Bye-bye."

Klassenarbeiten

AUFGABE 1 **S. 49**

1. Robert **isn't** late.
Is Robert late? No, he **isn't**.
The Dixons **are** at home.
Are the Dixons at home? Yes, **they are**.
2. My grandparents **haven't got** a car.
Have you grandparents **got** a car? No, **they haven't**.
3. I **don't have** (not) milk in my tea.
Do you **have** milk in your tea? No, **I don't**.

AUFGABE 2 **S. 49**

Lösungsvorschlag:
name: My name is Andrea.
country: I am from Germany
age: I am 12 years old.
hair / eyes: My hair is brown and my eyes are green.
brothers and sisters: I have got one brother and one sister.
hobbies: My hobbies are snowboarding, swimming and horseriding.
pets: I have got a dog. I don't have a pet.
favourite singer / band: My favourite singer is Robbie Williams.
favourite book: My favourite book is "Harry Potter and the Prisoner of Askaban."
favourite colour / s: My favourite colours are green and blue.
likes: I like music and computer games.
dislikes: I don't like Latin and maths.

AUFGABE 3 **S. 50**

My dad often does the washing-up.
When do you do your homework?
He doesn't watch television in the evening.
When do you go to bed?
I am not tired.
Has she got a bike?
Andrew hasn't got a bike.

AUFGABE 4 **S. 50**
Peter doesn't play with his cat.
When does school start?
They have a break at nine o'clock.
Do you like chocolate? – Yes, I do.
Don't forget your CD-player.
I don't do sports on Saturdays.

AUFGABE 5 **S. 51**
My name **is** Rebecca McLoyd. I **am** fifteen years old and I **am** a pupil at Hillmorton High School in Christchurch, New Zealand. Christchurch **is** the largest city on New Zealand's southern island.
My family **is** very big. I have got two sisters and a brother. The girls **are** twins. They **are** four years old and really cute. My brother **is** seventeen. He **is** terrible.
My friends **are** Jamie, Matt and Annika. Jamie and Matt **are** from New Zealand, too. Annika **is** from Germany. She **is** an exchange student. We all **are** friends.

AUFGABE 6 **S. 51**
Is Rebecca from Australia? No, **she isn't**.
Are the twins 7 years old? No, **they aren't**.
Is Annika from Germany? Yes, **she is**.
Are the twins from Christchurch? Yes, **they are**.
Is Rebecca a friend of Michael? No, **she isn't**.
Is Annika Rebecca's friend? Yes, **she is**.

AUFGABE 7 **S. 51**
Has Rebecca got two sisters? Yes, she **has got** two sisters and she **has got** a brother, too.
Have Jamie, Rebecca and Matt **got** a friend from Denmark? No, they **haven't**. They **have got** a friend from Germany.
Are Matt and Jamie brothers? No, they **aren't**. They **are** friends.

AUFGABE 8 **S. 52**
Grandma Elizabeth has got a pet, but she hasn't got a computer, a bike and a mobile phone.
Mr King has got a computer, a bike and a mobile phone, but he hasn't got a pet.
The twins have got a computer, a pet, a bike and a mobile phone.
Rebecca has got a computer and a mobile phone, but she hasn't got a pet and a bike.

AUFGABE 9 **S. 52**
Lösungsvorschlag:
In my free time, I read books.
In my free time, I play the violin.
In my free time, I don't do homework.
In my free time, I don't work.

4 Zeiten

ÜBUNG 1 **S. 54**
to carry: I carry, he carries
to miss: I miss, he misses
to catch: I catch, he catches
to say: I say, he says
to listen: I listen, he listens
to take: I take, he takes
to buy: I buy, he buys
to fly: I fly, he flies
to play: I play, he plays
to come: I come, he comes
to watch: I watch, he watches
to cry: I cry, he cries
to arrive: I arrive, he arrives

ÜBUNG 2 **S. 54**
Lösungsvorschlag:
We always eat breakfast at 7 o'clock. I often take the bus to school. Peter sometimes forget**s** his homework. She usually meet**s** some friends on the bus. He never go**es** to school on Sundays.

ÜBUNG 3 **S. 55**
Every Friday, Mrs Smith **picks up** her daughter Emma from school. Then they **do** the shopping together. They **go** to a big supermarket outside the city. Mrs Smith and Emma always **buy** fruit, milk and eggs. They **go** to the cashier and **pay** for their shopping.
In the afternoon, Emma **does** her homework. Then she **calls** her friend Mary. And on Friday evenings, Emma often **goes** to the cinema with Mary.

After shopping, Mrs Smith usually **goes jogging** in the park. Later her husband **prepares** dinner. In the evening, Mr and Mrs Smith often **watch** a TV film together.

ÜBUNG 4 **S. 55**

Lösungsvorschlag:

I like my friends, but I don't like maths.
I like sunshine, but I don't like rain and cold weather.
I like Christmas, but I don't like school exams.

ÜBUNG 5 **S. 56**

Lösungsvorschlag:

Liz likes chocolate, but she doesn't like fish.
Liz likes books, but she doesn't like computer games.
Liz likes pop music, but she doesn't like hardrock.

ÜBUNG 6 **S. 56**

Does Hannah live in Michigan?
Does school start at 6 o'clock every morning?
Do Hannah and her friends eat lunch in the cafeteria?
Does she play the violin?
Do Hannah and her friends sometimes go shopping at the weekends?

ÜBUNG 7 **S. 56**

Laura plays her violin every day.
Lilly is feeding the rabbits.
Simon doesn't like to do homework.
Look! The cat is chasing the dog!
Last summer, we went to Spain.

ÜBUNG 8 **S. 58**

Dad **is preparing** lunch.
Lilly **is doing** her homework.
Bob and Peter **are repairing** the bike.
Grandma **is cutting** the carrots.
Grandpa **is working** in the garden.
Laura **is playing** the violin.
The neighbour **is reading** a book.
Michael **is playing** football.
Kim **is watching** TV.
Susie the cat **is sleeping** on the sofa.

ÜBUNG 9 **S. 58**

X	V	R	S	A	W	A	B	C	D	H	I	J	C	K	Q	T	U	Z
A	H	U	R	R	Y	I	N	G	F	M	N	Q	L	U	V	W	G	H
O	D	S	D	R	F	E	L	M	G	R	S	R	E	A	D	I	N	G
B	T	X	Y	I	Z	A	A	B	M	C	C	T	A	H	R	O	P	I
P	E	D	I	V	K	L	N	X	A	U	V	W	N	I	I	Q	R	J
P	U	T	T	I	N	G	Y	Z	K	S	F	G	I	J	V	M	N	L
C	E	O	A	N	A	B	T	S	I	T	T	I	N	G	I	K	P	Q
Q	O	P	C	G	U	V	E	D	N	H	I	J	G	K	N	L	R	U
R	D	E	F	W	X	B	B	C	G	K	L	M	N	O	G	S	T	K
A	A	V	W	X	B	F	G	Z	H	B	W	R	I	T	I	N	G	I
G	Y	Z	A	S	T	O	P	P	I	N	G	F	A	G	H	L	M	H

ÜBUNG 10 **S. 59**

The girls are listening to music at the moment.
Peter is eating cornflakes for breakfast right now.
The boys are repairing their bikes at the moment.
Look! The bus is not/isn't stopping at the bus stop.
The cat is still sitting in front of the goldfish bowl.
The boys are playing football in the garden at the moment.

ÜBUNG 11 **S. 59**

1. It is Monday morning. Sandra Summer usually **goes** to school on weekdays. But today she **is staying** at home because she **has**
a bad headache.
2. Mrs Summer usually **works** three days a week in a bookstore. This week, however, she **is working** five days because her boss is on holidays. She **is** just **selling** a book to a woman with a baby.
3. On Wednesdays, Mr Summer often **plays** a football match with his colleagues from work. Today is Wednesday, and at the moment, his team is **leading** the match by three goals.
4. Sandra's CD-player is broken. Mr Summer **is repairing** it now. Sandra **cannot/can't help** her dad.
5. Sandra's brother Peter sometimes **writes** a letter to his grandma. Right now, he **is talking** to her on the phone.
6. It is Friday. Sandra **is** at school. She **is writing** a maths test at the moment. Sandra **is** tired, but she **must not go** home yet.

7. Mrs Summer usually **reads** a book on Saturdays. But today she **is watching** TV because it's the Queen's birthday.

ÜBUNG 12 **S. 60**
siehe unten

ÜBUNG 13 **S. 62**

to play → played
to listen → listened
to talk → talked
to smile → smiled
to hurry → hurried
to live → lived
to plan → planned
to carry → carried
to like → liked
to start → started

ÜBUNG 14 **S. 63**

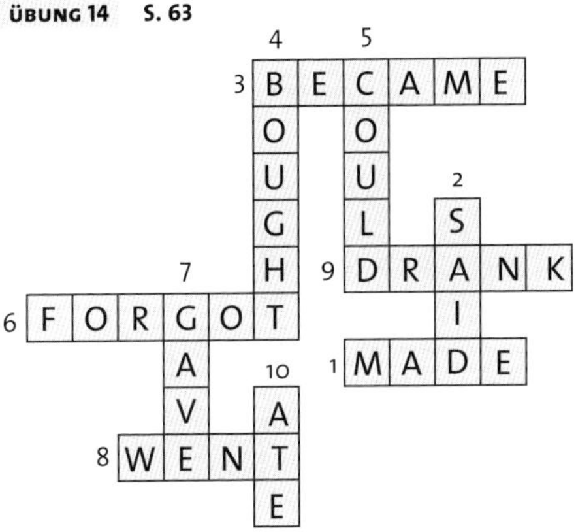

ÜBUNG 15 **S. 63**
Once upon a time there **was** a man who **married** a woman who already **had** two daughters. The man also **had** a daughter. Her name **was** Cinderella.
Soon after the wedding everything **went** wrong. The two daughters of Cinderella's new mother **got** all the presents, but Cinderella **worked** all day: she **washed** the dishes, **cleaned** the house and **made** the beds.
But one day, the King's son **gave** a ball. Cinderella **went** to the ball and **danced** with the Prince. The two other daughters **were** very angry. But Cinderella and the Prince **fell** in love, and soon they **married** and **lived** happily ever after.

ÜBUNG 16 **S. 63**
Yesterday, Liz and her mother **went** into town. They **took** the bus. On their way they **saw** a car accident. The police **were** already there.
Liz and her mother **got off** the bus in front of a big department store. They **bought** two T-shirts and a jacket for Liz and a small present for daddy's birthday next week.
On their way home, they **stopped** at a supermarket. They **went** in and **got** potatoes and lettuce for dinner. Then they **walked** home and **had** dinner with the whole family.

ÜBUNG 12

	verneintes *simple present*	verneintes *present progressive*
we talk	**we don't talk**	**we aren't talking**
they listen	**they don't listen**	**they aren't listening**
you run	**you don't run**	**you aren't running**
she eats	**she doesn't eat**	**she isn't eating**
they sit down	**they don't sit down**	**they aren't sitting down**
I com	**I don't com**	**I'm not coming**
we start	**we don't start**	**we aren't starting**
I swim	**I don't swim**	**I'm not swimming**
he drives	**he doesn't drive**	**he isn't driving**

Klassenarbeiten

AUFGABE 1 **S. 64**
(siehe unten)

AUFGABE 2 **S. 64**
Yesterday was Michael's birthday.
At the moment the cat is sitting on the sofa.
Look! The train is coming.
We visited Grandma last weekend.
Debbie usually reads a good book at the weekends.

AUFGABE 3 **S. 65**
The dog **is waiting** for its food.
The mother **is feeding** her baby.
The children **are running** home after school.
Grandfather **is sleeping** on the sofa.
Our teacher **is driving** a big car.
We **are dreaming** of long holidays.

AUFGABE 4 **S. 65**
Peter **likes** bikes, but he **doesn't like** cars.
My mother **drinks** tea, but she **never drinks** coffee.
Liz has got three rabbits and a horse, but she **doesn't** have got crocodiles.
Kim likes weekends and holidays, but she **doesn't** like Mondays.

AUFGABE 5 **S. 65**
Mr Smith usually **gets up** at 7:30 a.m. Now it is 8 o'clock and he **is** still **sleeping**.
Maggie often **plays** with her two sisters, but today she is home alone. So now Maggie **is watching** TV.
Nick usually **does** his homework in his room. But today he can't go home because he has lost his key. So he **is doing** his homework at school.

AUFGABE 6 **S. 66**
he sleeps; it is raining; you are; they are stopping; she came; he is being; they played; we swim; I am reading; you drank

AUFGABE 7 **S. 66**
Mr and Mrs Smith usually get up at 6 o' clock.
At 7 o'clock, Mr Smith walks to the bakery.
Mrs Smith wakes up Emma and Liz at 7 o'clock.
At 7:30 a.m., Emma and Liz get up.
The Smiths have breakfast at 8 o'clock.
At 8:30 a.m., Mr Smith goes to work.

AUFGABE 8 **S. 67**
The children **are playing** football.
Sarah **is copying** her math homework.
The teachers **are talking** to each other.
Peter **is reading** a book.
Mary **is eating** a sandwich.

AUFGABE 9 **S. 67**
"Little Kingston" **is** a small village.
My grandparents **live** on a farm there.
The sun **is shining** today: the horses are on the meadow.
The cat **is sleeping** in the sun.
Everyone **knows** each other.
Last week, a circus **gave** a show there.
At the moment, grandfather **is painting** the stable and grandmother **is cooking** dinner.
I **like** "Little Kingston".

AUFGABE 1

Infinitiv	3. Person Singular simple present	2. Person Plural present progressive	1. Person Plural
to hurry	he hurries	you are hurrying	we hurried
to say	he says	you are saying	we said
to listen	he listens	you are listening	we listened
to watch	he watches	you are watching	we watched
to play	he plays	you are playing	we played

AUFGABE 10 **S. 67**
My dad doesn't live with us.
Jim invites Mary for his birthday.
Maggie gets up at 6 o'clock every day.
I like dogs and cats.
My mum is preparing dinner at the moment.
Peter likes playing football.

AUFGABE 11 **S. 68**
Every Sunday, the Millers **get up** late. Then they **have** a big breakfast. After breakfast, Mr and Mrs Miller usually **go** outdoors. In summer, they often **go** biking. In winter, they go **hiking**.
Their daughter Victoria **doesn't like** biking. After breakfast, she usually **reads** a book. However her sister Liz **enjoys** outdoor activities. On weekends, Liz often **goes** climbing.
Today is Sunday, but it **is raining** cats and dogs. The Millers are at home. Mr and Mrs Miller **are watching** a DVD, and Victoria **is talking** to a friend over the phone.

AUFGABE 12 **S. 68**
Does Megan study in California?
Do the Millers go outdoors every Monday?
Are Hannah and her friend preparing dinner in the kitchen?
Does Lilly play the piano?
Do Hannah and her friends enjoy listening to music together?

AUFGABE 13 **S. 69**
Last summer, Lisa and her friend **spent** two weeks by the seaside. They **went** swimming every day. They **got** a good tan. They **met** nice people. They **ate** ice-cream every day. Every night, they **had** dinner in a different restaurant. One day, they **rented** a surfboard and **tried** surfing. They **had** a lot of fun, but after two weeks the holidays **were** over. Lisa and her friend **packed** their suitcases and **went** home.

AUFGABE 14 **S. 69**
Who wanted to overtake a boy? Mr Bond wanted to overtake a boy on his bike.
What did Mr Bond suddenly see? Mr Bond suddenly saw a big truck in front of him.
Why did Mr Bond crash into a tree? Mr Bond crashed into a tree because he was driving too fast.
Who called the police? The truck driver called the police.
What arrived some minutes later? Some minutes later, an ambulance and the police arrived.

AUFGABE 15 **S. 70**
Lily's mother: "Listen! The phone **is ringing**. Lily, can you **answer** it, please?"
Lily: "This must be Kim … Hello, Kim! How **are** you?"
Kim: "I **am** fine, thank you. Listen, let me tell you a story. Last Sunday, we **went** to the countryside. My grandparents **live** on a farm. We often **visit** grandma and grandpa at the weekends."
Lily: "What **do** you usually **do** there?"
Kim: "Oh, there **is** always a lot of work on a farm. Every morning, grandpa **feeds** the horses, for example. And grandma **milks** the cows. And I always **help** them when I **am** there."
Lily: "**Do** your grandparents really **have** horses, too?"
Kim: "Yes, they **do**. And I usually **ride** a horse when I **am** there. But listen, yesterday I **fell** off the horse and broke my leg. I can't go to school today!"
Lily: "Oh dear! Poor Kim! Listen! I **am coming** over right now, okay?"
Kim: "Okay! See you soon, then."

AUFGABE 16 **S. 70**
I go to school every day.
Mother is cooking lunch at the moment/right now.
Susie doesn't like apples.
Look! The taxi is arriving!
We were in Australia three years ago.
Lily's birthday was yesterday.
Now Betty must do her homework.

5 Präpositionen

ÜBUNG 1 **S. 72**

at three o'clock
on Monday
in the morning
on Wednesdays
at night
in summer
during lunch
at the weekend
on 15th October
at Easter
after breakfast

ÜBUNG 2 **S. 72**

Paul: "Hello, this ist Paul speaking."
Alex: "Hello, this ist Alexander. How are you?"
Paul: "I'm fine, thanks."
Alex: "I don't know. Is it nicer **in** summer or **in** winter?"
Paul: "Hmm, why don't you visit us **at** Christmas?"
Alex: "That's not a good idea. I always spend Christmas with my parents, my grandparents and my brother and sister. Let's meet **at** Easter."
Paul: "Great. We can have a big Easter egg hunt **in** the morning. **At** lunch we usually have a big meal together and **in** the evening we can go to the cinema."
Alex: "That sounds wonderful. Our holidays start **on** Monday 29th March. What's the weather like **in** March?"
Paul: "It can be sunny, but it also rains quite a lot **in** spring. That's our typical English weather."
Alex: "Well, I'm looking forward to seeing you **in** 2010. (...)

ÜBUNG 3 **S. 73**

We have a big brunch at the weekend.
My friend and I play hockey in the garden in the afternoon.
I walk to school in the morning.
I love to visit my grandmother in London in December.
My parents and I go to Italy in autumn.

ÜBUNG 4 **S. 75**

siehe S. 17

ÜBUNG 5 **S. 76**

Tim: "Mum, I can't find it. I looked everywhere **in** my room and it's not **in** the kitchen, either. It's not **on** the shelves and not **in front of** the coffee maker. I even looked **behind** the fridge."
Mum: "What are you looking for?"
Tim: "My mobile phone. Maybe it's stolen."
Mum: "Don't be silly! You often lose things, don't you? I think I saw it somewhere **in** the living-room, **next to** the television or on the table **between** the TV guide and my new book. I have an idea! I'll call you on your mobile phone and then we will know where it is."
Tim: "Ah, there it is! I left it **in front of** the mirror in the hall! Thanks, mum!"

ÜBUNG 6 **S. 76**

Now the pens are not next to the pencil case, they're in the pencil case.
Now the comics are not on the bed, they're next to the bed.
Now the clothes are not on the chair, they're in the wardrobe.
Now the CDs are not under the chair, they're on the bookshelf.
Now the poster is not behind the bed, it's above the bed.
Now the teddy is not under the window, it's on the bed.

ÜBUNG 7 **S. 78**

H	C	Q	Y	W	E	O	G	T
A	G	A	I	N	S	T	O	H
L	U	C	B	N	T	D	N	R
O	V	R	D	L	T	O	T	O
N	D	O	W	N	B	O	O	U
G	X	S	K	J	T	S	D	G
P	A	S	T	N	V	N	A	H
S	Y	R	O	U	N	D	I	D
Z	W	S	B	W	K	X	V	M

ÜBUNG 8 **S. 78**

Vincent: "Excuse me, could you please tell me the way to the train station?"
Mr O'Neal: "Oh, that's easy. You just walk **down** Mill Street until you get **to** the river. At the river you turn left and walk **along** it for 100 yards. Then you walk **across** a bridge and go straight ahead. Walk **past** the post office and **into** a small park. Go straight **through** the park and as you come **out of** it, you will see the train station."
Vincent: "That sounds very difficult."
Mr O'Neal: "Well, if you get lost, just ask for the way **to** Hill Park."
Vincent: "Okay, thank you very much, Sir. Bye-bye."

ÜBUNG 4 **S. 75**

Klassenarbeiten

AUFGABE 1 **S. 79**

1. A ball on a table.

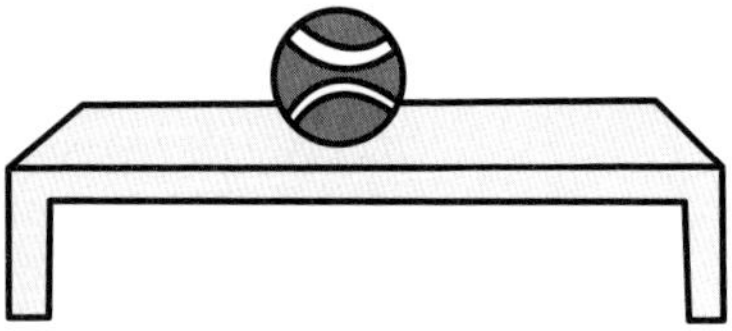

2. A ball under a table.

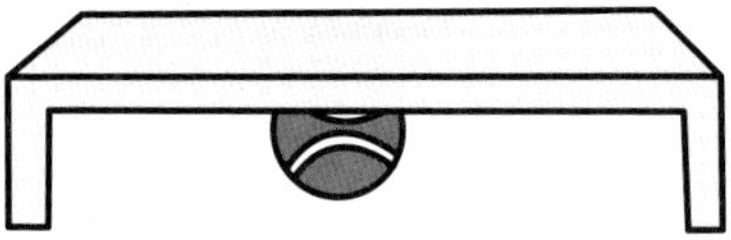

3. A ball between two tables.

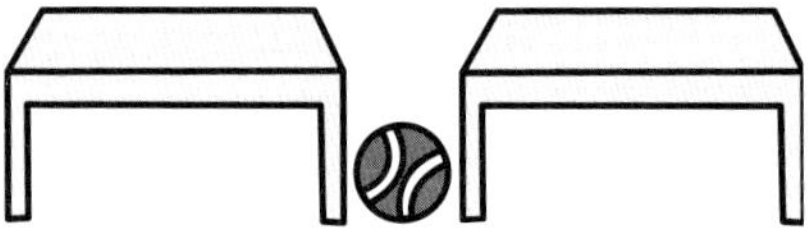

4. A ball next to a table.

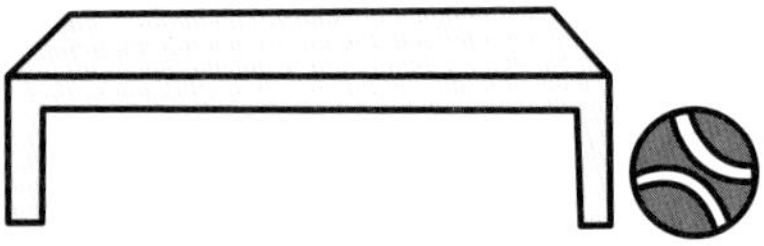

AUFGABE 2 **S. 79**

an Weihnachten → at Christmas
um drei Uhr → at three o'clock
nachts → at night
am Dienstag → on Tuesday
im März → in March
im Winter → in winter
zwischen ein und zwei Uhr → between one and two o'clock
am Morgen → in the morning
vor dem Abendessen → before dinner
während des Frühstücks → during breakfast
am Wochenende → at the weekend
2009 → in 2009

AUFGABE 3 **S. 80**

um ... herum → round
über → across, ins → into
hinter ... her → after
auf → onto
Von → from
gegen → against
aus → from
nach → to
aus → out of
vorbei → past, auf ... zu → towards
zu → to

AUFGABE 4 **S. 80**

My room is above the kitchen.
Jane's room is next to the living room.
The bathroom is opposite Jane's room.
Our cat Kitty sleeps on the sofa or in her basket.
There's a garden in front of our house.
There's a garage behind our house.
We live near the library.

AUFGABE 5 **S. 81**

Don't throw things **against** the window.
Are you **from** New Zealand?
My grandparents are walking **through** the garden.
Our dog usually jumps **onto** the living room table.
The plane **to** New York leaves Frankfurt at 8 a.m.
I can swim **around** the lake in 30 minutes.
Dad takes his little girl **to** school every morning.
Flo is riding his bike **down** the hill.

AUFGABE 6 **S. 81**

at	in	on
home	a bus	page 25
the bus stop	London	the table
school	the kitchen	book cover
the doctor's	the fridge	the right
	Mary's room	the wall

AUFGABE 7 **S. 81**
Where's my ruler? Oh, I see. It's **in** my bag, not **in** my pencil case.
Mm, but my exercise book is not **in** my bag. Oh, I can see it now. It's still **on** my desk.
That's strange. The flowers are not **on** the window-sill, but **in / on** the cupboard.
Well, and where's the cat? Oh, it's hiding **under** the sofa.

AUFGABE 8 **S. 82**
My bedroom is nice: I've got plenty posters **on** the wall. My wardrobe is **next to** the door. I've got a blue carpet **on** the floor. There is a big bookshelf **next to** my bed. There are many books **on** the shelf. My bed is **opposite** the door.
I've got a large mirror **in** my room, too. **In** the mornings, I often stand **in front of** it, to comb my hair.

AUFGABE 9 **S. 82**
Peter and Mary are friends. They both live **in** Kingston. Mary gets **to** school **on** foot. Peter gets **to** school **by** bus. Mia gets **to** school **by** bike. She always stops **at** traffic lights. Of course, she has lights **on** her bike.
After school, the children don't go home. They meet **at** the school playground and play volleyball together.

AUFGABE 10 **S. 82**
My mother is in her office.
Uuuh! Something is climbing up my leg!
Please sit down.
Mary fell off her bike.
Your English book is lying on the kitchen table.

6 Wortstellung

ÜBUNG 1 **S. 85**
My name is Julie Clark. I live in Nottingham. I am ten years old. My father works for a big computer company and my mother is a teacher. I have got two sisters, Liz and Anne. My sister Anne is twelve years old. My sister Liz is only six months old. We have got a dog, too. His name is Frank. My birthday is in March. I like the many presents. And we eat a lot of sweets on that day.

ÜBUNG 2 **S. 85**
Sarah likes to read books until she gets tired.
Linda writes a letter before she goes to the cinema.
Sandy gets good marks because she is clever.
When the sun goes down, it usually gets dark, too.
Rachel doesn't have a pet because she has allergies.

ÜBUNG 3 **S. 86**
Lily does not / doesn't do the homework in the classroom.
Lily cannot / can't watch TV in the classroom.
At school, Tom waters the flowers, so Lily does not/doesn't water the flowers in the classroom.
Lily does not / doesn't read a book in the classroom.
Lily has not got / hasn't got a rug in the classroom.
Lily does not / doesn't like the classroom.

ÜBUNG 4 **S. 87**
(Hier sind mehrere Kombinationen möglich, das direkte und indirekte Objekt kann jedoch nur an der hier genannte Stelle stehen!)
The shop assistant sells the lady an expensive coat.
The mother takes her sick child to the hospital.
The teacher shows his class an interesting picture.
She takes her little sister to nursery school every morning.

The girl tells her mother a lie.
Uncle Rudolf sends me an e-mail every month.
The policeman shows the old lady the way.

ÜBUNG 5 S. 89
usually, never, always, often, sometimes

ÜBUNG 6 S. 89
never → often
often → never
always → sometimes / usually / often
usually → never
sometimes → usually / often / always
never → often/always

ÜBUNG 7 S. 89
We always go swimming on Saturdays.
We often eat a lot of ice cream in summer.
Our English teacher never forgets to give us some homework.
Tina usually goes to the supermarket on Tuesdays.
Anne and Amy sometimes visit their mother together.
Mr Hope always helps his wife in the evening.
Laura and Hanna always meet their friends on Saturday evenings.

ÜBUNG 8 S. 90
Charly usually gets up at 7:30 a.m.
Mrs Parker often sings in the rain.
Tim's father never sleeps on the sofa.
Anne and Carole often buy cool clothes at that shop.
Anne is always hungry.
Sarah often goes shopping on Saturdays.
Grandma often prepares lunch for the whole family.
The teacher takes his pupils to the new museum next Monday.

ÜBUNG 9 S. 91
My parents go to work at 8 o'clock every day.
Our teacher travels to Madrid in Spain in summer.
Hanna does her homework at the desk in her room.
My mother goes shopping in the big shopping centre in town every Friday.
The school bus stops at the bus stop at 7:15 a.m. from Monday to Friday.
The children often go swimming at a big sports centre in town in summer.

ÜBUNG 10 S. 91
The school bus leaves the bus station at 7:30 a.m.
My family usually travels to England in summer.
Susie's mum goes to work from Monday till Friday.
Carole and Paul often go to the cinema at the weekend.
My sister Hanna meets her friends at the youth club on Saturdays.

ÜBUNG 11 S. 93
Help your brother with his homework. – Come in. – Shut the door. – Sleep well. – Have a good time. – Stop this terrible noise.

ÜBUNG 12 S. 93
Don't listen to music in the classroom.
Don't fight with your classmates.
Don't talk to your neighbour.
Don't eat during lessons.

Klassenarbeiten

AUFGABE 1 S. 94
Take out your books, please.
Open the books at page 32, please.
Read the complete text.
Use a pencil and underline everything that is important.
Answer the questions.
Look at the pictures in your books, please.
And please don't talk.

AUFGABE 2 S. 94
Mr Smith usually teaches English and history.
Lily sometimes eats cornflakes for breakfast.
Many children learn English at school.

We sometimes go to the countryside on Sundays.
The children never interrupt their teacher.
David and Gordon usually play tennis at school on Mondays.
Mrs Taylor usually drinks two cups of coffee every morning.
The children always do their homework in the afternoon.

AUFGABE 3 **S. 95**
The Hunts live on a farm. They have a lot of work because the animals need a lot of food.
Mrs Hunt loves the farm because she likes fresh air.
When the weather is fine, the animals are happy.
Their dog loves the farm, too, but the cat doesn't like it.
Mr Hunt likes his farm because he enjoys the countryside.
It's raining. Mr Hunt takes the horses into the stable until the sun comes out again.

AUFGABE 4 **S. 95**
What's for homework, please?
Can you spell the word "house", please?
Hurry up.
I play tennis every Friday.
Our teacher travels to England every summer.
Do not lean out of the window.
Don't worry.
Don't be so lazy.
Let's have a party on Saturday.
Can you say that again, please?
Sleep well.

AUFGABE 5 **S. 96**

Adverbien der Häufigkeit	Zeitangaben	Ortsangaben
never	after lunch	in the playground
usually	on weekdays	in the bathroom
often	at 7:30 p.m.	at home
always		

AUFGABE 6 **S. 96**
Mary never forgets her homework.
Laura always visits her grandmother on Sundays.
Mrs Cooper usually goes swimming on Wednesdays.
Simon often goes biking in the afternoon.
The caretaker usually locks the school gates at 10 p.m.
Bill sometimes reads a book.
John never clears the table.

AUFGABE 7 **S. 97**
Peter **doesn't have** a nice bike.
The twins **don't have** a pet spider.
Lilly **doesn't share** a room with her sister.
My grandparents **don't have** a big house.
Stephanie and Shelley **don't have** a cool mum.

AUFGABE 8 **S. 97**
Mrs Smith goes to work every weekday from 8:30 a.m. till noon.
Megan and Michelle go to school in Monrovia, California.
Christy and her children are going to the cinema in Los Angeles next Sunday.
Shelley moved to Hawaii last June. / Last June, Shelley moved to Hawaii.
The bus arrives at the school gates every morning at 8:15 a.m.

AUFGABE 9 **S. 97**
Can you repeat that, please?
We usually go to Spain on holidays every summer.
Mandy meets her friend at 6 p.m. at the youth club.
Come here, please!
I am sorry.
Which page are we on at the moment, please?

7 Fragen

ÜBUNG 1 **S. 100**

X	F	A	C	A	R	A	W	A	Y	S	T	M	E
A	B	W	C	X	E	W	H	O	S	E	E	F	G
B	W	H	E	R	E	X	H	E	L	P	X	T	I
W	H	E	D	E	A	F	G	I	H	J	W	B	E
B	A	N	A	W	H	Y	X	F	C	K	H	M	N
O	T	P	R	U	O	O	F	I	N	H	O	W	T
B	E	A	R	F	I	N	G	E	R	T	I	P	P

ÜBUNG 2 **S. 100**
Where does Caroline live?
Who are your teachers?
Why are they late?
What is your favourite colour?
Whose daughter is she?
When does school start?
Which house is yours?
How was school today?

ÜBUNG 3 **S. 101**
Where is London?
What is your name?
Where do you live?
Who is Mrs Miller?
What is your favourite colour?
How old are you?

ÜBUNG 4 **S. 101**
Who is Britney Spears?
What are mum and dad doing?
Where is Sydney?
What is dad doing?
What is Sally doing?
Where is Sally doing her homework?
Where are grandma and grandpa going?
What is a tsunami?
Who is Lily?

ÜBUNG 5 **S. 102**
Who has a violin lesson on Wednesdays?
What does mother read?
Where do the children play basketball?
What does Mr Smith own?
Where do we go to every Sunday?
Who likes chocolate?
When is Hanna's birthday?
Where is the post office?
Why do the children like their teacher?
Where does the Queen live?
Who enjoys the holidays?
Where does mother prepare dinner?

ÜBUNG 6 **S. 103**
Who's at school?
Who's doing their homework?
Whose shoes are these?
Who's very funny?
Whose house is the red house over there?

ÜBUNG 7 **S. 103**
What is Peter's favourite food?
How much is the museum entrance fee for a family ticket?
What colour is Bob's car?
What time is it?
Where do Peter and Tim live?
How many pupils are there in the classroom?
When does the post office open?
How often does our friend feed the rabbit?
What do I want to buy?
Who are our neighbours?
What is Susie's favourite thing?

ÜBUNG 8 **S. 104**
How many flowers are there in the garden?
How much is the book?
How many days are there in a week?
How many CDs have you got?
How much money has she got in her piggy bank?

ÜBUNG 9 **S. 104**
Whose white car is that over there?
What time is it?
How much are the apples?
Who is at work?
How many t-shirts has Mary got in her wardrobe?
Who is playing football?

ÜBUNG 10 S. 104

Vicky got £ 20 for her birthday. She wants to buy some toys.
Vicky: “Good morning. **How much** are these inliners, please?”
Shop-assistant: “The inliners are £ 15.”
Vicky: “Yippeh! So I’ve got £ 5 left. **What** else can I buy for £ 5?”
Shop-assistant: “Well, the stuffed animals are £ 4.95 each. **What** is your favourite animal?”
Vicky: “I really love cats. But I’ve got plenty of stuffed animals. **How much** is a computer game?”
Shop-assistant: “Mmm. Computer games are quite expensive. We don’t have one that is only £ 5. **Why** don’t you take a book?”
Vicky: “I usually go to the library. But **how much** is that jigsaw puzzle over there?”
Shop-assistant: “That jigsaw puzzle is £ 3.75.”
Vicky: “Okay, I’ll take that, too.”
Shop-assistant: “So that’s £ 18.75 all together. Thank you very much.”
Vicky: “Bye-bye.”
Shop-assistant: “Have fun with your new toys. Bye-bye.”

ÜBUNG 11 S. 106

Are you our new teacher? – No, I’m not.
Is London in Great Britain? – Yes, it is.
Is she nice? – Yes, she is.
Do you like your birthday present? – No, I don’t.
Does your mother work? – Yes, she does.
Can he swim? – Yes, he can.
Do you live in Sydney? – No, I don’t.
Is Sally doing her homework? – Yes, she is.
Is the door open? – No, it isn’t.

ÜBUNG 12 S. 106

Do you go to school by bike? – No, I don’t.
Is your car green? – No, it isn’t.
Are you from England? – Yes, I am.
Do you live in Germany? – No, I don’t.
Have you got a cat? – Yes, I have.
Isn’t mum nice? – Yes, she ist.
Can you read? – Yes, I can.
Are you reading a book? – No, I’m not.
Have you got two sisters? – Yes, I have.
Do you like school? – No, I don’t.

ÜBUNG 13 S. 107

1. Are there five T-Shirts in your wardrobe?
2. Is there a shoe in your wardrobe?
3. Are there four towels in your wardrobe?
4. Are there dresses in your wardrobe?
5. Is there a book in your wardrobe?

ÜBUNG 14 S. 109

Would you be quiet for a minute, please?
Would you open the window, please?
Would you like a sandwich?
Would you go to the cinema with me next Saturday?
Could you tell us the way to the train station, please?
I would like a cup of coffee, please.
Would you like another cup of tea?

Klassenarbeiten

AUFGABE 1 S. 110

Who’s that?
How old is she?
Where’s she from?
What’s her name?
What’s that?

AUFGABE 2 S. 110

When is the next train to London?
Where are your grandparents?
What colour are your trousers?
Whose bike is this?
Why is Mary in bed?
How much is this book?
Is Mike your brother?
How are you?

AUFGABE 3 S. 110

He is a good boy, isn’t he?
You are leaving tomorrow, aren’t you?
You have got a lot of money, haven’t you?
Pamela looks beautiful, doesn’t she?
Betty is your sister, isn’t she?
Grandmother lives in London, doesn’t she?
You can swim, can’t you?

AUFGABE 4 **S. 111**
Does Peter like biscuits? – No, he doesn't.
Does Peter like homework? – No, he doesn't.
Does Peter like holidays? – Yes, he does.
Does Peter like his friends? – Yes, he does.
Does Mary like biscuits? – Yes, she does.
Does Mary like homework? – No, she doesn't.
Does Mary like holidays? – Yes, she does.
Does Mary like her friends? – Yes, she does.

AUFGABE 5 **S. 111**
How many apples shall I buy?
How much does a DVD-player cost?
How many friends have got blond hair?
How many photos shall I take?
How many of you have got blue shoes?
How much does your baby weigh?

AUFGABE 6 **S. 111**
What is your favourite colour?
Excuse me, when is the next train to London, please?
Would you like an apple?
How old are you?
What's your name?
Who are you talking to?
Where is the exercise book?
How many T-shirts has Peter got in his wardrobe?
What time is it?
Penguins can't fly, can they?
Whose shirt is this?

AUFGABE 7 **S. 112**
Does Mary have a sister? – No, she doesn't. She has got two brothers.
Do the Miller's have an apartment? – No, they haven't. They've got a house with a garden.
Do you share a room with your sister? – No, I've got my own room.
Does Steven live in London? – Yes, he does.

AUFGABE 8 **S. 112**
When is the train to London? / **What time is** the train to London?
Are you thirsty?
Where are the twins?
How far is it from Berlin to Frankfurt?
What colour is your bag?
Why is she yawning?
What is Anne doing?
What's in the bag?

AUFGABE 9 **S. 112**
Is it raining? – No, it isn't.
Is Daddy at work? – Yes, he is.
Can you drive a car? – No, I can't.
Is this a dog? – No, it isn't. It's a cat.
Do you like reading? – Yes, I do.
Are you watching TV? – No, we aren't. We ...

AUFGABE 10 **S. 113**
She is a good mum, **isn't she?**
You don't have a lot of money, **do you?**
The dog is naughty, **isn't it?**
Your aunt lives in New Zealand, **doesn't she?**
They own a big house, **don't they?**
Your trousers are blue, **aren't they?**

AUFGABE 11 **S. 113**
Where is the bus station?
When does my mother get up every morning? / What time does my mother get up every morning?
Why is Mary wearing a cast?
Whose birthday is in January?
Who has a music lesson every Wednesday?
Which car is faster than the blue car?

AUFGABE 12 **S. 113**
How much is a flight to New York?
How much tea shall I buy?
How many sisters and brothers do you have?
How many pupils are in your class?
How much are these apples, please?

8 Zahlen, Uhrzeit und Datum

ÜBUNG 1 **S. 115**

23 → twenty-three
37 → thirty-seven
42 → forty-two
50 → fifty
55 → fifty-five
61 → sixty-one
70 → seventy
82 → eighty-two
90 → ninety
100 → a hundred
9 → nine
3 → three
13 → thirteen
28 → twenty-eight
34 → thirty-four
40 → forty
57 → fifty-seven
12 → twelve
81 → eighty-one
87 → eighty-seven

ÜBUNG 2 **S. 115**

5 – five, 15 – fifteen, 16 – sixteen, 21 – twenty-one, 25 – twenty-five, 38 – thirty-eight, 43 – forty-three
49 – forty-nine, 52 – fifty-two, 65 – sixty-five, 79 – seventy-nine, 84 – eighty-four, 91 – ninety-one, 100 – a/one hundred

ÜBUNG 3 **S. 115**

101 – a / one hundred and one, 243 – two hundred and forty-three, 335 – three hundred and thirty-five, 489 – four hundred and eighty-nine – 552 – five hundred and fifty-two
620 – six hundred and twenty, 791 – seven hundred and ninety-one, 804 – eight hundred and four, 910 – nine hundred and ten, 1000 – a / one thousand

ÜBUNG 4 **S. 116**

9th – ninth, 50th – fiftieth, 12th – twelfth, 1st – first, 22nd – twenty-second, 30th – thirtieth, 8th – eighty-eighth, 101st – one hundred and first, 3rd – third, 60th – sixtieth
24th – twenty-fourth, 32nd – thirty-second, 97th – ninety-seventh, 20th – twentieth, 73rd – seventy-third, 2nd – second, 11th – eleventh, 49th – forty-ninth, 52nd – fifty-second, 100th – hundredth

ÜBUNG 5 **S. 116**

siehe Seite 26

ÜBUNG 6 **S. 117**

ten, twenty, thirty, **forty**, **fifty**, **sixty**, seventy
forty-two, forty-four, forty-six, **forty-eight**, **fifty**, **fifty-two**, fifty-four
first, second, third, **forth**, **fifth**, **sixth**, seventh
sixty-five, fifty-five, forty-five, **thirty-five**, **twenty-five**, **fifteen**, five
seventh, sixth, fifth, **forth**, **third**, **second**, first
thirty-two, thirty-one, thirty, **twenty-nine**, **twenty-eight**, **twenty-seven**, twenty-six

ÜBUNG 7 **S. 117**

siehe Seite 26

ÜBUNG 8 **S. 117**

veneeents = seventeen
nnnoethounsaadinedtyenin = one thousand and ninety-nine
nvssiyteex = sixty-seven
thgeidnahunftyrrddeeeothr = eight hundred and forty-three
ttenwenniy = twenty-nine

ÜBUNG 9 **S. 118**

1. 1 + 5 = 6; 10 + 20 = 30; 7 + 4= 11;
100 + 25 = 125; 17 + 13 = 30; 34 + 26 = 60;
75 + 11 = 86; 14 + 30 = 44
2. 10 – 8 = 2; 100 – 89 = 11; 88 – 8 = 80;
54 – 40 = 14; 30 – 15 = 15;
90 – 16 = 74; 20 – 1 = 19; 79 – 27 = 52

ÜBUNG 10 **S. 118**

793056 ['sevn naɪn θriː əʊ faɪv sɪks]
5294113 [faɪv tuː naɪn fɔː(r) 'dʌbl wʌn θriː]
827501 [eɪt tuː 'sevn faɪv əʊ wʌn]
634577 [sɪks θriː fɔː(r) faɪv 'dʌbl 'sevn]

ÜBUNG 5 **S. 116**

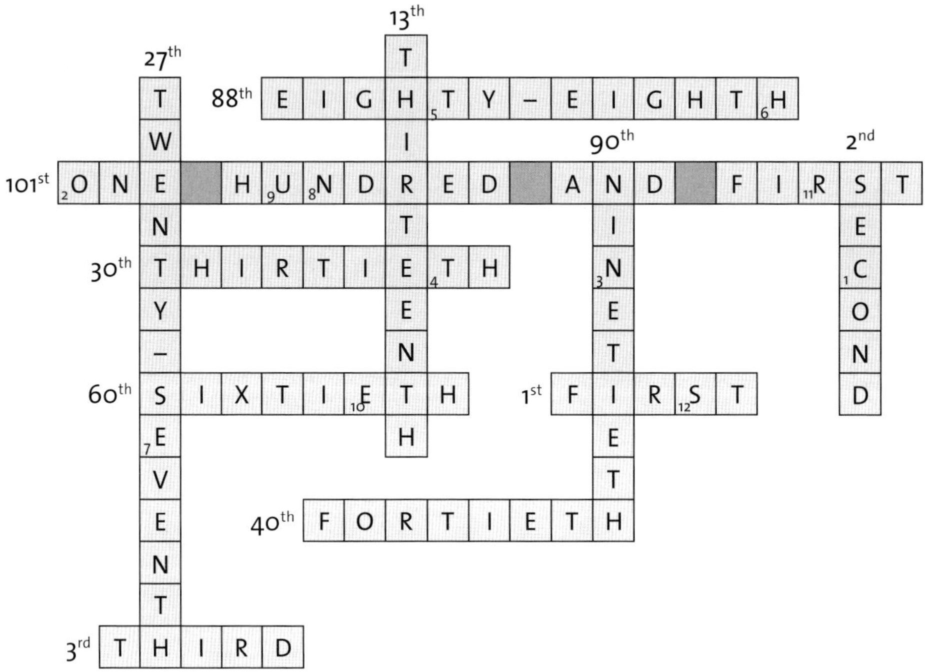

C	O	U	N	T		T	H	E		N	U	M	B	E	R	S
1	2		3	4		5	6	7		8	9			10	11	12

ÜBUNG 7 **S. 117**

+	seventeen	thirty-three	fifty-nine
seventeen	thirty-four	fifty	seventy-six
thirty-two	forty-nine	sixty-five	ninety-one
one hundred and eleven	one hundred and twenty-eight	one hundred and forty-four	one hundred and seventy
–	seven	eighteen	thirty-two
one hundred	ninety-three	eighty-two	sixty-eight
eighty-eight	eighty-one	seventy	fifty-six
sixty-five	fifty-eight	forty-seven	thirty-three

ÜBUNG 11 S. 121

1. It's six o'clock.
2. It's nine minutes past three.
3. It's five to nine.
4. It's twenty-five past eleven.
5. It's a quarter to six.
6. It's twenty past twelve.
7. It's half past nine.
8. It's two minutes past nine.

ÜBUNG 12 S. 121

It's five o'clock in the afternoon.
It's half past six in the evening.
It's ten to ten in the morning.
It's twenty-two minutes past ten at night.
It's twenty-five past eleven in the morning.
It's noon./It's midnight.
It's six minutes past six in the evening.
It's five to twelve in the morning.

ÜBUNG 13 S. 122

A	C	X	Y	T	T	S	R	V	W	S	A	T	U	R	D	A	Y
B	E	E	D	F	U	L	M	N	X	D	I	J	Q	X	T	A	Y
D	G	B	C	W	E	D	N	E	S	D	A	Y	M	N	D	O	M
F	A	E	R	P	S	C	D	F	G	H	I	A	J	N	K	L	R
S	R	O	H	Q	D	X	P	A	P	H	R	H	U	W	M	D	E
L	F	R	I	D	A	Y	D	M	N	O	P	S	I	N	F	G	H
M	N	F	D	G	Y	G	X	K	L	Y	A	E	F	H	I	A	L
A	D	F	D	X	P	H	H	S	D	T	H	U	R	S	D	A	Y
M	N	O	A	E	D	D	P	S	A	Y	F	G	Q	P	S	T	Y
G	M	H	I	M	O	N	D	A	Y	F	L	Q	P	A	B	C	D

ÜBUNG 14 S. 122

Then there's a break from twenty-five to ten till ten to ten. Susie has a history lesson from ten to ten to twenty-five to eleven. Then she has a geography lesson from twenty to eleven till eleven twenty-five. There's another (eine weitere) break from twenty-five past eleven till twenty-five to twelve. The German lesson is from twenty-five to twelve till twenty past twelve. Susie's last lesson, French, is from twenty-five past twelve till ten past one in the afternoon.

ÜBUNG 15 S. 123

Dear grandma,
Thank you so much for your letter. I am at school all morning from Monday to Friday. On Monday, I take the dog for a walk at five o'clock in the afternoon/at 5 p.m.
On Tuesday, I have got a piano lesson at half past three. On Wednesday, I stay at home in the evening and watch TV. On Thursday, I go to an extra arts class at a quarter past two. On Friday, I meet my friend Sarah in the shopping centre in the afternoon.
On Saturday, I go to the cinema with Paul at six o'clock in the evening/at 6 p.m. And on Sunday, I relax!
Love,
Jeannie

Klassenarbeiten

AUFGABE 1 S. 124

1.

2.

3.

4.
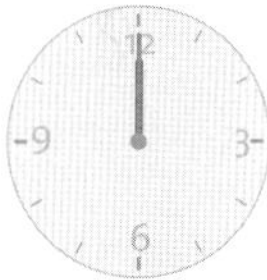

5.

6.

7.

8.

AUFGABE 2 **S. 124**
It's a quarter past six in the morning.
It's half past nine in the morning.
It's noon./It's midnight.
It's twenty-six minutes past two in the afternoon.
It's twelve minutes to four in the afternoon.

AUFGABE 3 **S. 124**
seventy-eight – one hundred and seventy – six – four – twenty-fourth

AUFGABE 4 **S. 125**
September the twenty-sixth – December the third – February the fifteenth – the first of April – the tenth of May – the twenty-fourth of June

AUFGABE 5 **S. 125**
The post office is open from nine o'clock in the morning till four o'clock in the afternoon from Monday to Friday. And it's open from nine o'clock in the morning till noon on Saturdays.
Dr. Smith's practice is open from eight o'clock till eleven o'clock in the morning and from three o'clock in the afternoon till six o'clock in the evening on Mondays, Tuesdays, Thursdays and Fridays. On Wednesdays, it is open from nine o'clock in the morning till noon.
Michael's supermarket is open from seven o'clock in the morning till seven o'clock in the evening every day.
The Indian restaurant is open only on Saturdays and Sundays from eleven o'clock in the morning till midnight.

AUFGABE 6 **S. 126**
Grundzahlen: seventeen, onehundredandeightytwo; ninety-nine; a thousand; sixty-two
Ordnungszahlen: fiftieth; second; forty-seventh; seventy-second; thirty-first

AUFGABE 7 **S. 126**
It is a quarter past four in the afternoon.
It is eight twenty-five in the morning.
It's noon.
It is a quarter to eight in the morning.
It is three fifty-two in the afternoon. / It is eight minutes to four in the afternoon.
It is four o'clock in the morning.
It is half past eleven in the morning.
It is sixteen minutes after nine at night.

AUFGABE 8 **S. 126**
1. It's two o'clock.
2. It's a quarter past seven.
3. It's 10 minutes to nine.
4. It's twenty minutes to eleven.

AUFGABE 9 **S. 126**
It equals / is ninety-three.
It equals / is fourteen.
Thirteen times five equals / is sixty-five.
It equals / is sixty-two.

AUFGABE 10 **S. 126**
Vicky's birthday is on the fourth of January.
Simon's birthday is on the twenty-second of March.
Grandpa Richard's birthday is on the twenty-fourth of April.
Mum's birthday is on the seventeenth of May.
Dad's birthday is on the thirtieth of October.
Grandma Elizabeth's birthday is on New Year's Eve.

AUFGABE 11 **S. 126**
The supermarket is open from 6 a.m. until 10 p.m.
My grandparents have lunch every day at noon.
The plane to New York is delayed for 35 minutes.
The piano lesson starts at half past three.
What time is it?

DUDEN

ISBN 978-3-411-72132-0